P9-DJA-322

MEDJUGORJE AND THE FAMILY

Helping Families to Live the Message

MEDJUGORJE AND THE FAMILY

Helping Families to Live the Message

Mark Miravalle, S.T.D.

Forewords by Fr. Svetozar Kraljevic, O.F.M.
and Fr. Michael O'Carroll, C.S.Sp.

Franciscan University Press
Franciscan University of Steubenville
Steubenville, OH 43952

Declaration

The decree of the Congregation for the Propagation of the Faith, A.A.S. 58,1186 (approved by Pope Paul VI on October 14, 1966) states that the *Nihil Obstat* and *Imprimatur* are no longer required on publications that deal with private revelations, provided they contain nothing contrary to faith and morals.

The author wishes to manifest his unconditional submission to the final and official judgment of the Magisterium of the Church regarding the events presently under investigation at Medjugorje.

Acknowledgments

I would like to offer my heartfelt thanks and appreciation to Fr. Giles Dimock, O.P., Sr. M. Regina Pacis, O.S.F. and Mr. Stanley Karminski for their astute editorial comments; to Fr. Michael O'Carroll, C.S.Sp. and Fr. Svetozar Kraljevic, O.F.M. for their generous support of the work; to Miss Patricia Doepker for her research and technical preparation of this work; and to my mother, Nora, my brother, Larry, my sister, Jeanne, and my grandmother, Luigia for being my first loving experience of family.

Cover Design: Art Mancuso

© 1991 by Mark I. Miravalle, S.T.D. All rights reserved.

Published by:
Franciscan University Press
Franciscan University of Steubenville
Steubenville, OH 43952

Printed in the United States of America

ISBN: 0-940535-33-5

Dedication

To Saint Joseph, Patron of all Christian Fathers,
and to my "Domestic Church":
my wife, Beth,
and our children:
John-Mark, Michael, Christiana,
Mariana, and Joseph.

Contents

Foreword

Mark Miravalle has undertaken a very important task in this very readable book. He has sought to penetrate the deep meaning of the messages diffused through the Catholic world from the Marian centre of Medjugorje, and to relate to this spiritual teaching the urgent imperatives of Catholic living at the present time. These imperatives are not new, indeed the author has the merit, in a time of change and excessive challenge, of picking out the essentials which endure, which may be called traditional in the valid and immensely valuable meaning of that word.

The overall context in some of the most perceptive passages is the Christian family. With great sensitivity and a certain justifiable originality, the author points to one aspect after another of what may be called "family spirituality." The sense of communion emanates from the documents of Vatican II, the Council which so insistently championed the dignity and rights of the human person. This is a striking paradox of the Christian message, that the maximum development of human personality is attainable within the living, emphasize living, framework of the Body. After the Master himself and his Blessed Mother, there are few more striking personalities in the Bible than St. Paul and he is the great doctor of the Mystical Body, the community par excellence. So Dr. Miravalle is in a great tradition in seeking to justify and advocate a spirituality of the family. It may be the call of the future.

As he points out convincingly and with ample detail there is a marvelous means of cementing this unity, this fellowship of the divine, in the Rosary. I liked especially his insistence on the basis of the mysteries in salvation history and his use of the Bible in this perspective.

One must give high praise to the exposition of the Mass, to the persuasive appeal to live the Mass. When I read him on objects of piety so often dismissed by moderns, I thought of St. Teresa of Avila and holy water. She wouldn't be without it. Forget not that outside the Bible she may be the most intelligent woman who ever lived; she is one of the great authentic mystics of all time.

A feature of Mark Miravalle's treatment of his various topics is the inter-weaving of apt quotations from papal pronouncements with excerpts from the Medjugorje messages. This will make his work a useful source-book. He also provides material for those who wish to encourage consecration to the Immaculate Heart of Mary and to the Sacred Heart of Jesus — what we have lost by the decline in these admirable, elevating practices! Here, as elsewhere, the decline has been arrested and the revival is on its way. Thank God for a courageous layman like Mark Miravalle. May he have many to make with him a great phalanx of knights of the Madonna.

Fr. Michael O'Carroll, C.S.Sp.
Feast of Our Lady of the Rosary
Blackrock College, Dublin, Ireland

Foreword

Dear reader, I ask you to give time to *Medjugorje and the Family*, for reading this book will be an investment that you will truly appreciate.

I first met Professor Mark Miravalle in Medjugorje in 1984. He was a doctoral student of Theology, with a thirst for theological discovery and in search of his own mission in the Church. I remember in these days for us at Medjugorje that the nights were not for rest, but for the long conversations we had walking the hill of the apparitions and the hill of the cross.

Medjugorje had the same meaning for Mark as it did for me; it was a return to the most profound things of faith and life, things we could now explore with greater depth and understanding. It was a return to the values learned in family life, to the values of our states in life, and even more a renewed search in discovering and appreciating the treasures of the Church.

This pilgrimage for Mark was at the same time a challenge, with a threat of the unknown, in the search of mission for himself, as well as in the name of those for whom he would later become teacher, writer, and head of family. In Mark's efforts to discover his mission for the Church, I heard unspoken, and yet in very clear words: "Holy Church, I have come to know you and love you, as well as my family. I want to serve you. Give me, please, a place and a mission in your heart. Open the ears of my heart that I may hear your heart, so as to serve you, to live according to your teachings, and to relate your teachings to others."

When asking about Medjugorje, the visionaries, or the message, Mark did not have any superficial curiosity, but he rather had an existential need to learn and know what was to become an integral part of his life mission for the Church.

The next time I encountered Mark, he was both the same person and yet different. At a Medjugorje Conference at which we both spoke, he came as a recognized lecturer and writer, as well as a professor of Theology from Steubenville University. He was received at the conference as a person of knowledge, wisdom, faith, authority, and commitment to the Church. The Church in America has in Mark Miravalle a model Christian in his vocation as theologian.

I would like to emphasize one very special dimension of this book as prophetic for our time. Dr. Miravalle is a very educated man, with a grasp of Theology that surpasses even that of many priests. But the respect he manifests for the priesthood, in its calling and mission, is far more than one could attribute to common courtesy. Mark reflects the love and respect that Our Lady has for the holy priesthood. This love and respect for the priesthood is especially important and prophetic for our times, for without this love for the priesthood, we will be ill-equipped to combat the spiritual persecution that faces the priesthood, a persecution which is ultimately a persecution of the Church Herself.

In this book, the reader will see Mark Miravalle as a believer, teacher, father, and husband. Parts of the book may appear intellectual, but it is precisely here that you, the reader, will receive your homework: to transform the words of the Madonna of Medjugorje into your life and the life of your family, so that *Medjugorje and the Family* becomes a means of a transfusion of faith right into your home.

Fr. Svetozar Kraljevic, O.F.M.
Medjugorje, Yugoslavia

This book has its origins in a series of talks on *Medjugorje and the Family* delivered at the Franciscan University of Steubenville.

The text has been fundamentally left in a transcribed form so as to facilitate the ''pick up-put down'' type of reading that so often must be used in the time demanding and interruptive atmosphere of daily family life.

Introduction

Originally the idea of writing a book on *Medjugorje and the Family* came as a response to the repeated comments of a fair number of parents who would say something to this effect: "We've heard of Medjugorje, we believe it is the Blessed Virgin, the Queen of Peace, and we know the most important thing is to live the message of Medjugorje. Now we've never prayed together as a family, we've never done any penance together as a family but we thought we'd try to live the *full message* of Medjugorje one Friday. The result was nothing less than disastrous. We tried to pray for the first time and got very irritated with each other at the lack of concentration and we had never fasted before but we attempted the full bread and water fast and we all got caffeine headaches. We tried to pray the Family Rosary and about halfway through we had to stop because we were so angry at the children because of their lack of attention and silence. At the end of our first day of trying to 'live the message of Medjugorje,' we felt cranky, discouraged, and much further from the peace of Christ than we did before we started the day. So now, we don't live the message of Medjugorje *at all*. We know it's truly the Blessed Mother and we often feel guilty about it, but we've concluded that this message must be only for priests, nuns and single people, but not for the family."

Comments like these, which can be joined to the best of intentions, also display a certain lack of prudence in incorporating the message of Medjugorje into that unity of persons known as "the family." And so, it seemed appropriate to attempt to provide some help in getting the message of Medjugorje into day-to-day family life.

Thus, the purpose of *Medjugorje and the Family* is to offer theological and pastoral guidance to families truly seeking to live the message of Medjugorje *as families*. It seeks, first of all, to add to an understanding of what we might call the heart of the message of Medjugorje, for to incorporate the message we have to know what the Blessed Mother is saying; and secondly, it seeks to provide some theological and pastoral principles for incorporating the message into that very sensitively balanced social phenomenon known as family life. This incorporation takes special pastoral sensitivity, along with some practical prudence, but it can lead to great family fruits, as well as avoiding much of the frustration and guilt manifested in the above-mentioned comments by parents.

I should also mention that the principles I am going to try to offer will be principles that can be applied to families of all different sizes and ages, but I will specifically try to highlight principles that will also work in families with young children. I do that with specific reason.

A couple of Mary's messages have specified bringing the very young into the prayer and sacramental life of the Church. She said on one occasion, "Bring the very young to Mass." And on another occasion she said, "Encourage the very young to pray." I had the opportunity to go over to Medjugorje on the June 25th anniversary this year, and one of the things the visionary Ivan stressed was that "you don't begin to teach your children how to pray at age 25." The family school of prayer and Christian life has to be a process. Children must be encouraged and must experience the atmosphere of faith from the earliest days. When this doesn't happen, parents can still make a positive effort to incorporate the message of Medjugorje into their family, even though the children are older. At the same time, I don't want in any way to detract from the importance of having a solid foundation from the beginning, and the benefit for children to have almost "by instinct" a disposition towards prayer and the sacramental life of the Church. Young children are very open to this for they love signs and symbols. Children are very well disposed to ritual and external signs. For example, if you start praying grace before meals, you will soon realize that you'll never get a bite again without having to pray grace, because the kids will remember even when you don't! They're much better in some ways than we are in maintaining the habits of Christian life once they have been firmly put into family practice.

Recently while giving a few talks on family life at Medjugorje, I spoke to a number of parents who felt the great wounds stemming from the fact that some of their children have left the Faith. Their cry was, "We've tried our best." There is no judgment that need be made on that here, and we always remember the great prayer of St. Monica and the tremendous efficacy of the prayer of parents for the spiritual state of their children, as well as noting the freedom of will and ultimate personal responsibility that each child must take for his own free choices made upon reaching adulthood. At the same time, we also don't want to take away the unquestionably solid fruit that comes from a loving and consistent early formation in the Faith.

So, while the principles should be applied to families of all ages, we need to have a special concentration on the young because Our Lady seems to be particularly concerned about starting children at a very early age in the life and the love of the Church in her words from Medjugorje. The importance of early formation, both spiritually and catechetically, for our children, is confirmed in the words of the Second Vatican Council on the *Declaration on Christian Education* where it says:

> It is particularly in the Christian family, enriched by the grace and the office of the sacrament of Matrimony that from the earliest years children should be taught

according to the faith received in Baptism to have a knowledge of God to worship Him and to love their neighbor (No. 3).

It is also worthy of mention, as we talk about Medjugorje and the family, that the Blessed Mother has declared 1990 as the "Year of the Family." She had previously asked 1989 to be specially dedicated to the youth and in an August message, she asked that 1990 be dedicated in a special way to the sanctification of the family. I believe this only confirms the appropriateness and need to focus on the theme of Medjugorje and family life.

We will not be directly discussing the questions that deal with the authenticity of the Medjugorje apparitions. There are a number of works on that subject. This work is rather for those who, while obediently awaiting the final and definitive judgment of the Magisterium, have themselves investigated the message and seek to personally incorporate the message into their family life. The freedom to do so reflects *authentic* Catholic theology regarding private revelation and is a Church-granted prerogative to every faithful Catholic.

The Church, in her history of dealing with private revelation, has taught that, in the case of a reported Marian apparition still under investigation, after a prudent examination of the message in light of the teaching of the Magisterium regarding faith and morals, as well as the concurring phenomena, we are free to accept private revelation and to live it, always with the readiness to conform our will to the final and definitive judgment of the Church.

We have seen this Church-granted prerogative clearly in the history of Marian private revelation, exercised for example at the apparitions of our Blessed Mother at Fatima. In 1917, Mary appeared under the title of Our Lady of the Rosary, and the visionaries Lucia, Francisco and Jacinta *immediately* incorporated the message of Fatima, and many of the 70,000 onlookers who saw the solar miracle also began to live the message of Fatima in 1917. They continued to live it until 1930 when the Church finally gave Fatima its official approval, indicating that there is nothing against faith and morals and, thereby, the faithful are free to live this message. Now, you wouldn't call Lucia, Francisco and Jacinta "disobedient Catholics" because they began to live the message of Fatima in 1917, before the official judgment of the Church, which did not come for another thirteen years. This would be most unfair and contrary to the mind of the Church. It's also interesting to note historically that when the final Church approval came through in 1930, the beautiful cathedral of Fatima was already half-built! There is need for caution and discretion, but at the same time, there is need for openness to the domain of private revelation which the Church Herself has. As Fr. Laurentin has noted, if the people (the *sensus fidelium*) didn't begin to acknowledge and even pilgrimage to a reported Marian site, then the Church would never have cause to step in to make its invaluable official judgment.

This freedom to accept a private revelation, even to pilgrimage to the reported location, is very clear in some of the comments that Pope John Paul II has made concerning Medjugorje, which have been documented on a number of occasions. To a number of Brazilian and Italian bishops, as well as to at least three American bishops, the Pope has said regarding Medjugorje: "It is good to go to Medjugorje to pray and to do penance." I have personally spoken and received confirmation of this fact from at least two of these three American bishops. To a Brazilian bishop, Bishop Murilo Krieger of Santa Caterina, who was pilgrimaging to Medjugorje and stopped off at Rome and discussed Medjugorje and his pilgrimage there with the Pope, the Holy Father remarked, "Medjugorje is a great center of spirituality." Bishop Paolo Hnilica, S.J., an auxiliary bishop of Rome (with the particular apostolate of journeying to the Eastern European countries in the name of the Church), has been to Medjugorje on three occasions, and on one of these occasions was asked by a group of pilgrims, "When is the Holy Father going to come to Medjugorje?". His response (which we have on video-tape leaving no question as to its authenticity) was: "The Holy Father told me that if he were not Pope he would already have been to Medjugorje."

These various statements of our Holy Father well reflect the freedom the Church allows regarding a contemporary apparition; they reflect prudence and caution, but also freedom and openness. With this spirit then, the very spirit of the Church, let us examine *Medjugorje and the Family*.

Chapter 1

Change Your Life in the Family

Dear children, I beseech you to start changing your life in the family. Let the family be a harmonious flower that I wish to give to Jesus. Dear children, let every family be active in prayer for I wish that the fruits of prayer will be seen one day in the family. Only in that way will I give you as petals to Jesus in fulfillment of God's plan. Thank you for having responded to my call (May 1, 1986).

The Madonna is clearly beseeching us to start changing our family lives. Now, every parent realizes that an attempt to change the sensitive balance of day-to-day family life can evoke from our families anything from minor grumbling to a domestic civil war! And yet the Blessed Mother is clearly asking us to change our family life which means a willingness to change our family routine where necessary for the sake of sanctifying our homes.

Universal Call to Change Family Life

The Blessed Mother at Medjugorje is not the only person asking us to change or re-examine our family life. There is a dramatically growing awareness throughout the world of the near universal need to begin to change our lives in our families.

Pope John Paul II, in his 1981 Apostolic Exhortation on *The Role of the Christian Family in the Modern World*, mentioned a few of the "shadows" that are hovering over contemporary family life today:

Signs are not lacking of a disturbing degradation of some fundamental values: a mistaken theoretical and practical

7

concept of independence of the spouses in relation to each other; serious misconceptions regarding the relationship of authority between parents and children; the concrete difficulties that the family itself experiences in the transmission of values; the growing number of divorces; the scourge of abortion; the evermore frequent recourse to sterilization; the appearance of a truly contraceptive mentality (No.6).

The Pope goes on to explain what is often at the root of this family breakdown:

At the root of these negative phenomena there frequently lies a corruption of the idea of and the experience of freedom, conceived not as a capacity for realizing the truth of God's plan for marriage and the family, but as an autonomous power of self-affirmation often against others, for one's own selfish well-being (No. 6).

The Holy Father is fundamentally saying that the basis of these domestic shadows is the clear misuse of the God-given gift of freedom. And you will notice, both the Blessed Mother and the Holy Father are making reference to *God's plan* in conjunction with freedom. In general, God has given us the freedom but we as families are not using this freedom to seek God's plan for marriage and the family, but rather for selfish, unfulfilling ends. The Holy Father exhorts families to "become what you are!" Become what God wants us to be, a communion of persons in love and in life, an image of the Holy Family, and ultimately of the Trinity Itself. The Blessed Mother is calling us to the same thing in Medjugorje: to make changes in incorporating God's plan for the family, the goal of which is very simple — its sanctification. She's calling for the sanctification of the domestic Church.

So, we've got the Blessed Mother from Medjugorje calling

for family change, we've got the authoritative teacher of the Church, the Holy Father, sounding the same call, as well as a statement from Mother Teresa of Calcutta that will be discussed later, pointing out that the peace of the world is first disrupted *in the home*. That's where the peace of the world loses its hold first. Anything that happens outside of the home, internationally or locally, that is bereft of peace can in some sense be traced to the home. These three contemporary voices are calling us to change our family life.

Some parents may respond to this Marian call for domestic change: "But that's not my family that the Holy Father described. We're not divorced, we've had no abortions, our kids go to Mass, there are no drugs, and occasionally we'll even pray the Rosary together. Is the Blessed Virgin still calling us to change our families?" To that question, I think it's important to look at the second part of what Mary says in the opening quote. She says: "Let the family be a *harmonious flower* which I wish to give to Jesus." A harmonious flower? I don't think even the most optimistic parent, if asked "What is the first image you think of in describing your day-to-day family life?", would confidently respond: "Why, of course, a harmonious flower." Personally, with five kids, the oldest seven and the youngest five months in the womb, I know that I could respond regarding day-to-day family life, "The presence of peace, yes; a harmonious flower, no!" I think it is possible that by using this expression, the Blessed Mother is telling us that the quest of family conversion, like the quest of personal conversion, is never fully completed in this life; it is an ongoing process. St. Augustine, commenting on Psalm 41, which refers to the "deer that yearns for running streams," says that man's thirst for God will never fully be satisfied in this life. Another quoted spiritual maxim says: "The extent to which you stand still in the spiritual life is the extent to which you fall back." Why? Because the spiritual life is a dynamism that's supposed to grow. And the extent to which it stagnates is the extent to which growth is hindered. So, too, regarding the spiritual lives of our families.

Domestic Examination of Conscience

The Blessed Mother is calling all families to what we can term a new *domestic examination of conscience*. The proper understanding of this phrase I think well captures Mary's call to the families of the present generation. She is calling parents and families to re-examine their present commitment to the Christian life. And I don't mean just the spiritual life, because the proper Christian life can also have major effects on the emotional, psychological, and even physical stability of family life.

It is possible that a few families, in making this new domestic examination of conscience, may conclude, "We are doing all that we can right now; we've firmly committed ourselves to family prayer and the sacramental life of the Church and we're doing the maximum our family can possibly handle." Please note that the Virgin Mary is not uniformly saying to families, "Double or triple your family prayer," regardless of where you are presently. Some families may truly be able to say, "We're at the tilt; we're really doing all we can in terms of generosity in prayer, penance, and the sacramental life of the Church." But I think it's also fair to say that the strong majority of families can say, "We could be more generous; we could be more committed; we could be more consistent in our family prayer."

An authentic domestic examination of conscience will usually lead to some hard decisions regarding domestic re-prioritizing. You can't have lasting change without re-prioritizing. For example, this will mean a prioritizing of Family Rosary over family television; family prayer over Nintendo or video shows or other activities that should rightly take second place to Our Lady's plan for the family which again is ultimately God's plan for today's family. The Blessed Virgin's message is a real challenge for our families, but in light of the ubiquitous domestic problems that are threatening the basic fabric of Christian family life today, as described in part by Pope John Paul II, Mary's call remains a very reasonable and attainable price to pay for the exchange of family demise for family peace.

A new, honest look at our family life ultimately leads us to this question: *Is there room for greater spiritual generosity in our family life?* And we'll examine the message in the following chapters to see exactly what she's calling for in terms of a positive change in family life.

Three Guiding Principles for Changing our Family Life

In this vein, I would like to offer three general guiding principles that may be of help in our effort to change our family lives through a deeper incorporation of the Madonna's message (even before we discuss the actual message itself). But let me emphasize that these would be only general guiding principles, for ultimately the final and appropriate decision of "how much how soon" to incorporate the Medjugorje message for each individual family must rest *with the parents*: the parents, in prayerful and prudent discernment, tapping the grace of the sacrament of Matrimony. Many of us have lost the full sense of the sacrament of Matrimony, as if it were a sacrament conferred on the day we were married and then ceased to be a channel of grace. No, the sacrament of Matrimony is an ongoing, efficacious sacrament that sanctifies the family. And that's why the ultimate decision of "how much how soon" must rest with no one else but the parents, because no one else knows the children like their own parents. Living the message of Medjugorje as a family relies strongly on the need for prayerful discernment and utilization of the sacrament of Matrimony in the family by the mother and father of each respective family.

Let me offer three guiding principles to help families to incorporate this message: first of all, the principle of "prudence according to our state in life;" secondly, the principle of "committed consistency;" thirdly, the principle of "generosity."

Prudence According to Our State in Life

Prudence has a number of meanings today. The classical meaning of prudence is "a practical wisdom in action, directing the person toward his or her final goal." The Blessed Mother, as we will see, is asking that holiness be the final goal of family life. First of all, in the area of practical prudence, I would like to stress the value of a *gradual incorporation* of the Madonna's message for families. This is especially true for families with younger children. If you note in the Medjugorje event, the Blessed Virgin did not start asking for the full fifteen decade Rosary, for two days of fasting, even for the Family Rosary in the first couple weeks. She, like a good pastor, gradually nurtured the parish there with the long-term goal of enabling them to be eventually more generous in prayer and penance. The long-term goal of domestic sanctification should likewise be approached gradually.

A prime example of the value of gradual incorporation of this message comes from the visionary Marija. Marija mentioned to me back in 1985 when we talked in our mutually substandard Italian (the only foreign language she could speak at the time) that when the Madonna first asked for daily praying of the seven Our Fathers, Hail Marys and Glory Bes, Marija thought to herself, "That's a lot of prayer for me each day." This also tells us that the visionaries were not necessarily at the height of sanctity when Mary first appeared. In fact, the visionaries once asked the Gospa, "Why us?" and Mary responded, "Because I don't always choose my best!" Then Mary asked for the five decade Rosary and Marija's response was the same. She said to herself, "How am I going to get five decades of the Rosary in each day?" Then still later, Mary asked for fifteen decades of the Rosary each day and, of a small youth prayer group in Medjugorje, Mary asked for at least three hours of daily prayer. And because of Our Lady's gradual spiritual guidance to the young people, Marija could turn to me in a state of profound peace and say, "But now I want to pray always." This principle is so clear in the physical world and yet it's such a mystery to us in the spiritual world: the principle and fruits of a gradual but committed incorporation. I have a friend, an old college buddy who runs the San Francisco Marathon every year. I said, "Hey, Jim, how do you do it running some twenty plus miles in a few hours?" He said, "Well I started with two miles and they got boring so I gradually increased it to five. Then I ran five miles daily for about six months and again felt the urge to run farther, so I boosted it up to eight. Then I heard about the marathon. So, I started training over a period of time, again increasing my distance to ten miles, and then twelve; after a long while, I was able to run the marathon." This is the beauty of the principle of gradual incorporation. Jim didn't start by running the marathon, and we as families have to apply this principle to the message of Medjugorje as well. Most of us can't start running the marathon of Medjugorje, and the full message can be like a marathon. It's a very challenging message. It is challenging because our Mother needs these prayers and sacrifices at this critical time in history. She needs our prayer and fasting for *our* sake. But it's a gradual incorporation that lays the best foundation for a family living of the message.

I often kid my friends in northern California that if people in California were as committed to prayer and the spiritual life as they are to jazzercise, aerobics, or their other physical routines, the whole state would be canonized! There's incredible commitment there. No matter how you feel that day, you get yourself to jazzercise, aerobics, etc. If we only had that kind of commitment to the spiritual life it would be phenomenal. So, it's the same principle we need in living the message: a gradual, but committed incorporation of the message, especially where the family is concerned.

Under this first guiding principle of prudence, let us also examine the need to incorporate the message of the Madonna *according to our state in life*. This is a very important principle, the most fundamental rule for spiritual direction which the saints discuss, namely, that Christian holiness is sought according to our God-given state in life. A prudent living of the message of Medjugorje is not going to do damage to a God-given state in life; rather, it's going to perfect and sanctify it.

I want to quote from St. Francis de Sales, the master on holiness for laity in the world, in his classic work, *Introduction to the Devout Life*. He uses the term "true devotion" for holiness but it's the same notion. First of all, he talks about holiness perfecting, not going against, our state in life. He says:

. . . True devotion does us no harm whatsoever but instead perfects all things. When it goes contrary to a man's lawful vocation, it is undoubtedly false. "The bee," Aristotle says, "extracts honey out of flowers without hurting them" and leaves them as whole and fresh as it finds them. True devotion does better still. It not only does no injury to one's vocation or occupation, but on the contrary it adorns and beautifies it. . . . Every vocation becomes more agreeable when united with devotion. Care of one's family is rendered more peaceable, love of husband and wife more sincere, service of one's prince more faithful, and every type of employment more pleasant and agreeable (*Introduction to the Devout Life*, Part I, No.3, Doubleday).

Applying the words of de Sales to Medjugorje, we can say that the message should be incorporated according to our state in life as a family member, and that also has to be the ultimate criterion regarding the question of "how much how soon" for ourselves and our families.

St. Francis de Sales further points out that Christian holiness is for all states in life but should be incorporated differently according to individual vocations. He says:

When He created things God commanded plants to bring forth their fruits, each one according to its kind, and in like manner He commands Christians, the living plants of His Church, to bring forth the fruits of devotion, each according to his position and vocation. Devotion must be exercised in different ways by the gentleman, the worker, the servant, the prince, the widow, the young girl, and the married women. Not only is this true, but the practice of devotion must also be adapted to the strength, activities, and duties of each particular person. I ask you, Philothea [a lover of God], is it fitting for a bishop to want to live a solitary life like a Carthusian? Or for married men to want to own no more property than a Capuchin, for a skilled workman to spend the whole day in church like a religious, for a religious to be constantly subject to every sort of call in his neighbor's service, as a bishop is? Would not such devotion be laughable, confused, impossible to carry out? Still this is a very common fault, and therefore the world, which does not distinguish between real devotion and the indiscretion of those who merely think themselves devout, murmurs at devotion itself and blames it, even though devotion cannot prevent such disorders (*Introduction to the Devout Life*, Part I, No.3).

How beautifully de Sales expounds on devotion as being a call for every state in life, but exercised differently according to the individual state in life, as well as the truth that holiness gets a bad name because of the indiscretion of those who seek to incorporate it outside of their state in life. So, too, can this happen with the message of Medjugorje. Holiness does not mean dressing in black with back hunched to the ground and never being able to laugh. That's not holiness. The Madonna has many times mentioned, "I want you to have a new joy in your life." The joy comes from the life that she calls us to in her Gospel message.

Committed Consistency

The second principle is a committed consistency. The idea is that the family must acquire what we call "virtus," strength, the disposition of the will in forming the good habit of family prayer. How does that happen? It happens through commitment and most importantly through recommitment to what our Mother is asking for.

Greek philosophers discussed the question: How do you acquire a virtue, a strength? They answered, you acquire it by repeating a desired act over and over. This clearly applies to the commitment of family prayer. There is the need for commitment and recommitment, and given the sensitive and human nature of family life there are going to be times of failing. And that's who Mary is coming for. She, like her Son, is not bringing this message to perfect, immaculately conceived families. She is coming to *our* families, imperfect families, families who don't live out the Christian life as generously as we could.

We are families who need the recommitment and the continual efforts to try to incorporate this call as a family virtue. A virtue is a disposition of the will towards good; it is a track of the soul that leads you to the good choice out of good habit. And that's what we want to instill in our family life: the disposition of our minds and hearts toward the family spiritual routine of prayer, fasting, and the sacramental life of the Church.

But under this second principle of committed consistency in terms of family life, we must also include the need for flexibility. When you are talking about children being involved, you must have flexibility in the structure of Christian family life.

Allow me to make an old philosophical distinction regarding the notion of "epikea," or the "spirit of the law." Plato and Aristotle had differing opinions on epikea. Plato thought that any exception to the law hurt the law. Anytime there was an exception we did damage to the law. Aristotle said rather, that whenever we are talking about a human law, epikea serves the law. The exception serves the law because the law can't encompass every human possibility. Now, this is not true of divine law, but it is true about human law. I think it is very important to incorporate the Aristotelian notion of epikea when we talk about the family spiritual life. For example, let us consider a commitment to the Family Rosary. You do have the commitment; you seek to pray it nightly, but on a given night guests come over. They stay late, and they don't happen to be of the disposition to join you in Family Rosary. The company leaves, it's late, (say eleven o'clock) and the children are tired. Do you then force the children to pray the Family Rosary, even though there would be a question as to whether they'd even be conscious? I think rather (and again this is up to the prayerful decision of the father and mother in utilizing the marriage sacrament), it might be more beneficial for them to be able to concentrate on either one decade of the Rosary, or to pray an Our Father, Hail Mary, and Glory Be at the end of the night or, even if the children are asleep, for the parents to pray the Rosary together. This way you keep the virtue, the habit of family prayer intact, but you use flexibility in what I think really better serves the family practice of prayer in the long run.

So, by consistency I do not mean an unreasonable rigidity which I don't think works well in the family life. I think it can harm the family in the final analysis. Exceptions are not opposed to a committed consistency. I think it's part of how that consistency practically works when you're talking about children. Although we also keep in mind that the exception should never replace the rule.

Generosity

The third principle for a family incorporation of the message of Medjugorje is the principle of generosity, especially in our own time. My first encounter with Father Svetozar Kraljevic, a priest at Medjugorje, back in 1984, well illustrates this point. We met at midnight one evening and spoke well into the morning. One of his first comments to me regarding the Madonna of Medjugorje was: "The poor thing is desperate . . . this Mother of God is desperate for our prayers." And that has always stuck with me because he said it with such sincerity and empathy for her maternal pain. Fr. Svet was right. She is desperate. But she's not desperate for her sake. She is the Queen of Angels and Saints. Theologically we say she is number four in the hierarchy of being, and when the three ahead of you happen to be divine, you're in a pretty good spot! So she's not coming down and calling us to new levels of generosity for her sake. It's obviously for our sake.

If we can't hear the call to change our family life from the Blessed Mother, from Pope John Paul II, from the words of Mother Teresa, then we can look at our own lives, the people close to our own family, if not in our family, that are living signs of the great crisis in family life today. Whether it be divorce, whether it be children on drugs, whether it be abortion, sterilization or any of these forms of domestic devastation, it's not something abstract, at a great distance from us. All of us know someone close who's experiencing the breakdown of family. Some of this is the bitter fruits that come out of the seventies generation. The seventies was the ''me'' generation. When you're worried about *me* it's awfully hard to think about *us*. And *us* translates into family life. So, too, we have the whole phenomenon of people who are not emotionally affirmed in our own age. The call to change our family lives seems to be a universal call and we've got evidence of it from all over. It is in this context that Mary is calling us to a new generosity.

As we will discuss at greater length under the theme of peace, the Madonna has said that these will be her last apparitions. How this is to be interpreted is difficult to say. The visionary Mirjana, has also said that chastisements would take place within her lifetime, the same type of chastisements we hear of reported as a strong possibility in the third secret of Fatima. For most of us, that also means in our lifetime. Even though it is ultimately a message of spiritual peace, there is also what I would call a *peaceful urgency* about the Medjugorje message. For this reason too, Our Blessed Mother is calling us to a new generosity. The goal is to try to be as generous as possible, first, in light of the fact that the Mother of God is calling us to be generous, and secondly, in light of our own examination of the crucial contemporary signs of the times.

Let me read this September 13, 1984 message answering the question why Mary continues to need this generosity toward prayers. She says:

Dear children, I continually need your prayer. You wonder what all these prayers are for. Turn around, dear children, and you will see how much ground sin has gained in the world. Therefore, pray that Jesus may win (September 13, 1984).

It is a need deeply centered on the fact that the Spiritual Mother who intercedes for us is calling on the world for the spiritual sacrifices she needs with which to intercede; she needs the prayer that leads to the sanctification of the family and the penance that builds up not only our own family, but also the entire Body of Christ.

Domestic Kenosis

Let me briefly mention a model of family life that I think can be of some help in the general incorporation of the Medjugorje message into family life. I call this family image the model of "Domestic Kenosis."

"Kenosis" is a Greek word meaning "the act of self-emptying," "to empty yourself," or "to sacrifice yourself." In Philippians 2, the great canticle of kenosis, St. Paul describes the ultimate kenosis or the self-emptying of Jesus Christ for our sake:

> Though he was in the form of God Jesus did not count equality with God a thing to be grasped, but *emptied Himself* [the reference to kenosis], taking the form of a servant, being born in the likeness of men. And being found in human form He humbled Himself and became obedient unto death, even death on a cross. Therefore, God has highly exalted Him and bestowed on Him the name which is above every other name, that at the name of Jesus every knee should bow, in heaven and on earth and under the earth, and every tongue confess that Jesus Christ is Lord, to the glory of the Father (Phil 2:6-11).

What does the example of Jesus' kenosis mean for family life? Simply put, all family members, according to their position or state or role in the family, must also empty themselves and personally sacrifice for the well-being of the family. They've got to imitate what Christ did for the universal family, and we've got to do it for our individual families as well.

We are called to take and accept the "domestic cross." I know in my own case, in my second year of marriage, that as husband and father, I really fled from the domestic cross with my own family. My wife, Beth, had given birth to our first child, John-Mark, and I found myself getting involved with more and more things outside of the house. I got involved in rugby on evenings and weekends. I took on more responsibilities at school. They were all decent enough things in themselves. I wasn't going out stealing and pillaging. But it finally dawned on me that I was really trying to leave the domestic kenosis of my family. I was really trying to get away from the self-emptying and self-sacrifice that my family needed, from the humility of changing diapers and being with kids who cannot converse with you with any great articulation or discuss the contemporary headlines of the day. I was really taking flight from my domestic cross. Rather, we are called to empty ourselves for the good of our families. Because when we empty ourselves, then we're going to share in the *resurrection and glory of family life* as well. We're going to share in the graces and the peace that come from that family sacrifice.

The particular process of domestic sacrifice will be different according to our state in life and family position. The father is going to empty himself differently for the family than the mother. Pope Pius XI in such a beautiful expression called the mother the "heart of the family." The father is the head, the mother is the heart, but both must empty themselves. Even the children (although in their early years it's very clear they need more receiving than giving) must also understand the principle that their personal good is secondary to the family good, that their individual desires have to come second to the common good of the family. It doesn't have to be understood intellectually but experientially in the family.

We are experiencing today on a very significant level the phenomenon of the single parent family. Is the Madonna's message to families not valid or applicable for them? On the contrary, it is most certainly and in a special way applicable to them. As Pope Pius XI discussed in his 1930 document on Christian Marriage (*Casti Connubii*), when the father fails to be true to his role as head of the family, then the mother is called upon to become both "head and heart" of the family. The same can be said of the need for the father to take on the mother's role as "heart of the family" when the mother fails to perform this kenosis for her family. This in no sense is intended to minimalize the heavy burden of one parent taking on the task of both head and heart, but the parent who has been providentially granted this exceptional domestic cross must be assured of Our Lord's and His Mother's special and accentuated graces in faithfully carrying out this call, and the single parent has all the more need to utilize the means of family sanctification to which the Madonna is focusing our attention like Family Rosary, Family Fasting, Family Reconciliation, and the other means we shall discuss.

The message of the Madonna in no sense excludes a call to single parent families, and personally, as a product of a single parent family, I see the message as a source of particular hope. and consolation for the parent who is called to be both head and heart of their domestic Church.

I think it's particularly important in our own age to stress the kenosis of the father for the family. We're experiencing what's being called "father deprivation" because the absence of the proper presence of the father, physically, emotionally, and spiritually, is being experienced so universally. When the father, as in my own personal example, flees from the domestic cross where his physical, active presence in day-to-day family life is much more of an abstraction than a practical reality, he does not incorporate the humble emptying of himself for his family into his life. In whatever other way there is emptying, it is not primarily a family emptying. This is a sad phenomenon of our age.

As John Paul II has said, the father has to have a visible role in the spiritual formation of the family. It's important that he be visible. And to be visibly present, he must be consistently *physically* present, normally on a daily basis.

Recently during his Sunday sermon, a local priest cited a survey regarding the relationship of parents' participation in church with that of their children. The results showed that when both parents regularly attended church, the possibility of their children, upon their reaching adulthood, carrying on the practice of regular church attendance, was seventy-five percent. If the father alone regularly attended church, the percentage of the children carrying on the practice dropped to fifty-five percent. But if only the mother regularly attended church, the possibility of the children carrying on the practice dropped to fifteen percent. That's a forty percent drop in the possibility of children regularly attending church if it is only the mother as compared with only the father. This confirms all the more the incredible impact of the father's religious practice and example (or lack thereof) on the future religious practice of the children.

One major psychologist said that the greatest impact on a young child was the phenomenon of seeing his parent pray. Why? Because at first, obviously the child doesn't understand precisely what's going on, but he does know that Mommy or Daddy is taking time out for this encounter. Secondly, Mommy or Daddy is talking to someone whom the child can't see, which intrinsically supports the fact that beings exist which you cannot see, spiritual beings, whether it be uncreated in God or created with the angels. And thirdly, Mommy or Daddy thinks so much of this that he or she does it every day. This is authentic Christian formation by example.

If we look at Ephesians 5, theologically the father is the image of Christ and the mother is the image of the Church. You may ask yourself then who should do the greatest sacrificing for the family, the father or the mother? This is a question that technically should not be asked since, as the Holy Father has said on several occasions, marriage should be a *mutual subjection out of reverence for Christ*. But if you were to ask who should do more for the family, I think a theological case could be made that it should be the father. Because the father is in the image of Christ and Christ unquestionably did more for His Church than the Church did for Christ. It would have to be the father who is called to the greatest emptying of himself for his family as priest, prophet and king of the domestic Church. And that's not just a platitude or a pietistic comment. It's truly the spiritual formation of the family through the domain of the service of the father. That is his first vocation. So, while all are called to do this domestic emptying in this very challenging Medjugorje message, I think we especially need to encourage paternal kenosis in our day.

Domestic Kenosis as a family model can really keep focused for us that to live the Christian life as families and to live the Medjugorje message as families, we must be prepared to embrace authentic Christian sacrifice. By trying to live this family model while incorporating the Medjugorje message in a practical way, we convey concretely to our children the great Christian principle, "To be self-fulfilled, you must self-deny." This is the contradiction of the Cross, the contradiction the world wants no part of, and the contradiction we should want every part of. It is the contradiction the Madonna is presently calling each family to in her invitation to "start changing your life in the family."

Chapter 2

Faith and the Family

Dear children, let your family be a place where holiness is birthed. Help everyone to live in holiness but especially your own family (July 24, 1986).

In a recent trip to Medjugorje, I heard Ivan comment that many people are out to make prayer groups, but he stressed that the first prayer group must be the family. Later you can expand the prayer group, but it's really a call to that family sanctification first: the Gospa calling for the family to be the first birthplace of holiness. We know that true holiness has its beginnings in a living dynamic faith.

Medjugorje Call to Faith

What, in essence, is Mary's call to faith at Medjugorje? She has, according to the visionaries, asked for a more resolute committed faith in God and in Jesus Christ, as the only mediator to the Father. There's only one way to get to the Father and that's through the person of Jesus Christ. She has asked for a greater commitment in faith. In fact, on the sixth day, Mary stated, "There is one God and one faith. Believe firmly." Secondly, she has asked for specific faith in the apparitions themselves. Vicka, on the third day, asked Mary for a miracle, some kind of sign (Mirjana was particularly concerned about people calling her crazy, so she was also in favor of some type of sign), and Mary responded, "Let those who do not see believe as if they see."

The Madonna further promised particular graces, special graces, for people who live and incorporate the message of Medjugorje before the time of a sign — some type of visible permanent sign on Podbrdo, the hill-site of the first apparition, to take place at the end of the apparitions. The sign is particularly for the "unbelievers."

The idea of a promised visible sign is sometimes seen as difficult to believe, but this is a well-known Marian precedent. Our Lady almost always gives some type òf physical sign, at least in the major universal apparitions. At Lourdes, in 1858, when she came as the Immaculate Conception, it was the sign of the miraculous spring. At Fatima, Our Lady of the Rosary, in 1917, granted the sign of the solar miracle to the 70,000 onlookers. Why a sign? Because we are physical beings. There is a concreteness to the faith. We have an incarnational Savior. He took on flesh, and in the Church, an extension of Him, there is also a domain of something physical, as we see in each of the seven sacraments, water, bread and wine, oil, etc. Mary has granted signs, in these major approved apparitions in the last 150 years. At Medjugorje also, she has promised some type of permanent visible sign at the end of the apparitions. This is most appropriate for beings made of both spirit and body, as long as we always keep in perspective that the sign is granted to encourage us to live the message and never as a "Barnum and Bailey" end in itself. Our Lord faced this difficulty in the Gospels where people loved the miracles but didn't want the conversion message of the Gospel. To multiplying the loaves to feed five thousand, "yes," said the crowds; but to the call to eat His body and blood in the greatest sacrament of Eucharist, most of the crowds said, "no."

Can we theologically justify Mary saying: "I will be able to intercede for greater graces if you incorporate the messages before the sign"? Is this theologically sound? St. Augustine's definition of faith is "to believe in what we do not see." Theologically, if, on prudent grounds, we do accept something of the faith without having to have a physical proof or sign of it, it is an indication of a greater and more meritorious faith. Of course we know this scripturally with St. Thomas the Apostle, who would not believe until he thrust his fingers into the side of Our Lord, and Our Lord responded: "Blessed are those who have not yet seen and yet believe" (Jn 20:29). So, yes, it can be theologically verified that if there are prudent grounds for belief before a granted sign, then it would merit an even greater degree of graces.

Let us keep in mind the classic definition of faith as defined in Vatican Council I in 1870. Vatican I says that faith is a supernatural virtue through which, by the inspiration and help of God's grace, we believe that what God has revealed is true. So, faith ultimately is God's gift to us that allows us to believe in what He has revealed and to believe that it is true. We are so utterly dependent on God that we could not even believe in His revelation without His help! And what has God revealed? God's ultimate revelation is the person of Jesus Christ. Therefore, Mary's call to faith is a call to accept the full revelation of Jesus Christ, in Himself and in His Body, the Church. To return with a new and permanent commitment to Jesus Christ is the heart of the Medjugorje call to faith.

The Family and Faith

How is this call to Faith practically incorporated into the family? The Blessed Mother has offered a few specific ways that strengthen family faith. She has asked for what I would term a return to the "domestic sacramentals." Let us look at this July 1985 message:

Dear children! Today I call you to place more blessed objects in your homes and that everyone put some blessed object on their person. Bless all the objects and thus Satan will attack you less because you will have armor against him (July 18, 1985).

We see here the importance of blessed objects. This simply re-iterates traditional Catholic faith in the value of placing something blessed on your person. Why? What is a blessing theologically? A blessing is having an ordained priest call God's special presence on a particular object. That then gives Satan a particular repulsion against the object. We know that even in the extreme case of exorcism the use of a blessed crucifix and holy water is effective in the process of casting off Satan. The Madonna seems to be summoning us to return to the practice of having blessed objects in the home and on our person. She calls it "spiritual armor" which implies its strong and real ability to protect spiritually. It is a beautiful and profound way to talk about the need for blessed objects. I should also mention that if you begin to have your children wear blessed objects, like medals, scapulars, or crucifixes, then you almost have to take on the domestic job of jewelry repair, especially if we're talking about young boys. You put the medal on the child with great care, and three minutes later during the front yard pick-up football game, you see the Marian medal go flying through the air, and then you make the dive to try to catch it before it hits the ground! Nonetheless, there's still the beauty of having children wear blessed objects, and children do enjoy the sacramentality, the physicality of being able to wear and touch something with God's special presence upon it.

Holy Water

The Gospa has also called for a return to the use of holy water. She has asked for a return to the practice of using holy water specifically in the home. One of the things very young children enjoy the most about going to Mass is putting their hands in the holy water font. And regardless of what type of strange, "innovative" sign of the cross they perform on themselves, they enjoy that physicality. It's important to remember the beauty of sacramentals. St. Thomas Aquinas said that the sacramentals of the Church lead us to the sacraments. Why do we bless ourselves with holy water? Because when we bless ourselves with holy water in the name of the Father, Son and the Holy Spirit, we are affirming our Baptism. We are saying "yes," "credo," "I believe," again. The sacramentals that the Blessed Virgin is calling for, blessed objects and holy water, don't stop with themselves but they lead us to the sacraments, the seven Christ-instituted channels of sanctifying grace. There is also the benefit of having things close that Satan is repulsed by, for he could never enjoy material things with the special presence of God. It's just common theology. It just makes domestic sense.

Religious Art at Home

Other fruitful types of domestic sacramentals that can add richly to the atmosphere of faith at home include the use of religious art or holy pictures. It is often true that the art found in the home reflects the priorities of that home. Art is usually an expression of the loves and joys of the family. The visible presence of the images of the Sacred Heart of Jesus, the Immaculate Heart of Mary, St. Joseph, Patron of the Universal Church, as well as pictures of patron saints and holy angels (who often appear with the Blessed Mother during the apparitions) brings these members of the Body of Christ alive in the hearts of our children. The idea of having religious objects and religious art in places of honor throughout the home where the children can regularly see them can only foster family faith. In the Middle Ages, many Catholics learned their catechism by walking through the cathedrals and looking up at the images and Gospel events portrayed in the stained glass windows. And looking at the central mysteries of faith depicted in Christian art, they learned the essential truths of our faith. In a sense, we can offer our families a visible catechism as a vehicle of faith in our homes. The generous use of religious images in the home is certainly well implemented by the families of St. James Parish in Medjugorje. Thanks be to God, my wife has more prudence than I do with regard to accomplishing this because if it were left to me I would have icons and holy pictures every five or six inches on every wall in the house!

Visible Bible and Family Altar

This message of October 1984 bespeaks the value of having the Bible placed in a central visible place in the home:

> Dear children! Today I call on you to read the Bible every day in your homes and let it be in a visible place so as always to encourage you to read it and to pray (October 18, 1984).

The Madonna asks us to have the Sacred Word of God in some visible place. Notice the practicality of the Blessed Mother, to put the Bible in someplace visible, so you're more disposed to reading it and praying it as a family. And I think a corollary to this, although not specifically in the message, but certainly practiced in Medjugorje, is to have a family altar. Having a place set aside, a visible place where the family prays together is most valuable. We're incarnate beings, and it helps the habit of family faith to have a place set aside particularly for offering prayers and spiritual sacrifices. It doesn't have to be extravagant but something that assists the notion that here is the place where we as a family pray regularly.

The idea of a family altar is important theologically in the sense that we as a domestic Church should be offering spiritual sacrifices to the Father. In his first Epistle, St. Peter calls us to become "a spiritual house, to be a holy priesthood, to offer spiritual sacrifices to God through Jesus Christ" (1 Pet 2:5). We, the laity, should be offering spiritual sacrifices in light of our priesthood, which is not an ordained priesthood, but a priesthood that should likewise offer sacrifices. And what is an altar? An altar is a place where we offer a sacrifice. There's a great fittingness to having a place designated in the house for the offerings of prayer and sacrifices of the domestic Church and as a reminder to pray.

If possible, the family altar should be a place with a designated mantle, shelf, or table, which is embellished with holy pictures, statues, the Word of God, and candles. Candles richly symbolize Jesus as the light of the world and are helpful in keeping the children visibly focused on the altar during family prayer. Several families have used the practice of turning out the lights and lighting only the candles, which assists the children in blocking out all other possible sense distractions. They look either into the pitch dark or at the family altar. This is especially helpful with very young children even if they do not recite all the prayers themselves.

Faith by Osmosis

Let me summarize the Gospa's family call to faith by the expression of "Faith by Osmosis." These things which Mary is calling us to use in our homes — holy water, blessed objects on our persons and in our homes, the family Bible in a central place, and the corollary and the practice at Medjugorje, of having a family altar — are all directed to establishing an atmosphere of faith at home. But all these domestic sacramentals put together are not nearly as important as the foundation for an authentic atmosphere of faith in the home; namely, the concrete example of faith and prayer as manifested *by the parents themselves*. It is very easy for children to recognize the incongruity between what parents say and what parents do. A woman once mentioned, "Every time my daughters come over I ask them why they don't pray the Rosary. They just don't want to have anything to do with it." Someone else then asked the woman, "Have you ever prayed the Rosary with them or said, 'I'm praying the Rosary now, would you like to join me?'" This concrete example of prayer seems to be far more fruitful in evoking participation than most anything else. The greatest invitation for children to join in the faith life of the family is the daily and loving concrete witness of parents. Like nothing else, that seems to be the avenue of conveying this Medjugorje call to faith into our domestic Churches.

Let me conclude with a quote from Pope John Paul II, from his document on the Christian Family, that I think very well brings home, and with a type of magisterial certainty, the fruits that we can expect from this domestic life of faith. We've talked a lot about sacrifice, and I've really tried to be clear on the fact that there is a sacrificing, a re-prioritizing, and that means a renewed domestic kenosis for everybody. But there are also tremendous domestic fruits from this sacrifice, and we'll speak more of those priceless fruits in the final chapter on *Peace and the Family*. But let's look at the Holy Father's comments about the irreplaceable position of parental example in the quest for faith and also a foretaste of its sublime fruits:

> The dignity and responsibility of the Christian family as the domestic Church can be achieved only with God's unceasing aid, which will surely be granted if it is humbly and trustingly petitioned in prayer. . . . The concrete example and living witness of parents is fundamental and irreplaceable in educating their children to pray. Only by praying together with their children can a father and a mother — exercising their royal priesthood — penetrate

the innermost depths of their children's hearts *and leave
an impression that the future events in their lives will
not be able to efface* [emphasis added] (No. 59-60).

I want to emphasize that last line, "and leave an impression
that the future events in their lives will not be able to efface."
The Holy Father here isn't speaking against the possibility of
free will, but I think he's trying to say precisely where we can
place our family trust and hope. These are not fruitless efforts.
We can really trust and count on the effects of the irreplaceable
position of family example. As the Pope says, the impression
of dynamic family faith, as accentuated by the faith example
of parents, will have such a significant impact on the hearts of
our children that the many difficulties of life's long journey
will not be able to remove it. This embodies a statement of
great consolation for parents. There is a real sense of resting
in the peace that comes from faith in the family.

The Medjugorje message of faith is a return to God with
greater commitment, a renewed belief and love of Jesus Christ
and His Body, the Church. And in a real, concrete way, it's a
call to incorporate into our home life an atmosphere of dynamic
faith that, by osmosis, tells our children that the Christian home
is a living and active part of the Body of Christ; a domestic
part that is truly living, loving, growing, and believing.

Chapter 3

Prayer and the Family

Dear children! Today I call you to the renewal of prayer in your homes. The work in the fields is over. Now devote yourselves to prayer. Let prayer take the first place in your families (November 1, 1984).

This reference of the Blessed Mother to prayer taking first place is probably the most pivotal question that parents and families must ask themselves. Can we truly say that prayer is the first priority in the family? Now that appears to be a rather routine question but it is really a very cutting question. It is asking whether family prayer is ultimately more important than work, than school, than finances, than family recreation, than television, etc. That doesn't mean that all those things are bad in themselves. Certainly to be a responsible family we have to incorporate many of these things. Rather, the Blessed Mother is asking, "Is prayer the *first* priority of the family?" That's a hard question but one that every family must honestly ask themselves: "Can we say that at least we're trying to have prayer as the first priority of our family?" This is not just a "spiritual" concern, for, if prayer is not the first priority, it's going to affect concretely the very relationship of family life. That means the relationship between parents and children; it means the relationship between the children themselves; it means the relationship between children and their friends and even their experiences at school. It's a central, fundamental question. To the degree that we answer "no, family prayer is really not our first priority," theologically then, we must admit we are to that degree removing the possibility of God sanctifying the family. It's as if we are

34

striving to build family holiness and family peace, but we've got a gaping hole in the foundation.

For many of our families, "the work in the fields" is never over. The Blessed Mother's message is now that the field work is over, make prayer your first priority. For many families, the "field work" of life is never over in our lifetime, and family prayer never makes it to the top of the list of domestic priorities. There can always be some reason posed in preventing family prayer from reaching the number one position. Our Lady knows this is possible especially in our age, because our age is the first age that we can be entertained at almost every moment of our life. We can wake up to the radio, we and our families can watch away the day with television and Nintendo. We can even put on the walkman headsets during almost any conceivable intermission of events. We can literally end the day without a single moment of silence. Technologically, this is the first age when this is so. Other eras necessarily had moments of silence where we were forced to think about the possibility of God, the fundamental meaning of life, and the most basic question, "What is the purpose of our earthly existence?"

Again, the Blessed Mother is not calling us to irresponsibility in terms of the other domestic needs. She's simply asking what is the priority? It is sad that so many families, in the final analysis, would have to respond that the field work is never over and that the priority of prayer never makes it to the top. It may be the third or fourth priority, or maybe it gets in the top ten, but it's never the first priority. One possible sign of prayer priority is on those frustrating days when we seem to get nothing else done *but prayer*. Do we then go to bed thinking that the day was wasted or that the day was counter-productive because none of the things on our check list got done except the fact that we prayed as a family? We should rather say that at least the first family priority was taken care of today. At least the most important thing of the day was achieved, and that was that we prayed as a family. Our effort at home, however humble, however failing at times, should be to try to strive to make family prayer our first priority.

The Nature of Prayer

What is prayer that the Blessed Mother is so concerned with it as a daily occupation, as a priority of each day, for individuals and for families? There are a number of classical definitions of prayer. The one most often used in catechisms is the definition of St. Thomas Aquinas (which he actually takes from St. John Damascene): prayer is the "raising of the mind and the heart to God." It's a good definition because it talks about both elements of the human soul: the intellect and the will, the mind and the heart. St. John of the Cross, in a slightly different way, defines prayer as "a loving awareness of God." That's a little more experiential. But I think the definition of St. Teresa of Avila, the "Doctor of Prayer," is the most fitting. She says prayer is a "conversation with Him who we know loves us." Look at the premise we start with in prayer. We're not speaking to a stranger, we're speaking to the "Abba," which is not properly translated "father" but rather "papa" or "daddy." We're starting prayer in this comforting context of communicating to Someone who loves us infinitely. God loved us first, and we in prayer respond to His already existing love for us.

No wonder the Blessed Virgin asks prayer to be our first priority for families, to begin each day in loving conversation with God. First of all, we should pray so as to find out and discern for the family each day God's will which we know changes, especially in the fragile situation of family life. Secondly, the family prays to ask for the graces to be able to live out God's will for each day. And thirdly, I think especially for parents, we pray for the grace and the wisdom to be able to adjust to God's manifest will during the day, which can oftentimes be surprising. Remember God's will as it appeared to the Blessed Virgin. She wasn't sitting around waiting for the archangel Gabriel. And yet Gabriel came, and it was a surprise, but the way the faithful Virgin reacted is the way we're supposed to react to such surprises of God manifesting His will in our own day. Oftentimes it's a surprise. And I question how prepared we can be for the surprises that are part of daily family life without beginning the day with prayer and nurturing the day in prayer. The grace to first know God's will, and then to accept it, can only be received by consistant daily prayer. So, it doesn't seem to be an unreasonable request that the Blessed Mother is asking for in making prayer a personal and a family priority, especially when the fruit of such prayer is perduring family peace.

At Medjugorje, Mary has invited all family members to pray. This April 1986 message beautifully includes all members of the family from the young to the elderly:

> Dear children, you are forgetting that you are all important. The elderly are especially important in the family. Urge them to pray. Let all the young people be an example to others by their life and let them witness to Jesus. Dear children, I beseech you, begin to change through prayer and you will know what you need to do (April 26, 1986).

We see here the notion of every family member having a crucial importance in domestic prayer. In our own age, there is a growing awareness of the need for grandparents to try prudentially but actively to evangelize or catechize their grandchildren. Tragically and for various reasons, the faith of the grandparents has not been passed on through their own children to the grandchildren. It's tragic to hear the pain and suffering experienced by grandparents whose grandchildren have not been baptized and have not been formed in the faith. But there should always be trust in the fruits of having the grandparents take a new spiritual responsibility in praying for the spiritual state of their grandchildren. Sometimes the fruits are not always seen right away. But there is great strength in the prayer of parents for children and of grandparents for grandchildren as well. So, the importance of the "elderly" is something our culture seems to be missing more and more, and the special gifts of the elderly for the family is alluded to in the Gospa's message.

"Encourage the Very Young To Pray"

The Blessed Mother has also asked the "very young" to pray. In a March 1985 message, she said: "Today I call you to renew prayer in your families. Dear children, encourage the very young to pray and to go to Holy Mass" (March 7, 1985). We've already mentioned the need of starting, from the earliest years, the atmosphere of faith and prayer that encourages young children to pray. It is true of many families where there is consistent daily prayer (specifically the Rosary) that the children see their participation in prayer as part of the family responsibility just as much as setting the table for dinner, cleaning their rooms, etc. They soon ask when, for example with the Family Rosary, they can start leading their own decade. Of course, we get all different kinds of formulations of the Hail Mary from the little ones, each with their own "unique version." But nonetheless, they want to know when they can be allowed to do what the rest of the family does. And, thus, they learn to pray. So, again, Our Lady is very strong on the very young and I'll again mention the importance of the very young when we talk about what Mary says should be the center of our lives — the Holy Mass.

Praying Together as a Family

The Madonna has especially called family members to pray together, for families to pray *as families*. In this July 1989 message given to Ivan she says:

> Dear children, your Mother asks you who are present tonight, when you return home, [to] renew prayer in your family. Take time for prayer, dear children. I as your Mother, especially want to tell you that *the family has to pray together*. The Holy Spirit wants to be present in the families. Allow the Holy Spirit to come; the Holy Spirit comes through prayer. For this reason, pray and allow the Holy Spirit to renew you, to renew today's family. Your Mother will help you [emphasis added] (July 3, 1989).

Family prayer is the vehicle allowing the Sanctifier, the Holy Spirit, to enter into the family to accomplish the task of the Sanctifier in each family, which is to make our families holy domestic Churches. Directing the family towards sanctification comes through prayer; that's the avenue. And on a more personal level, I know in our own family, before the Medjugorje phenomenon, I certainly prayed, went to Mass and said the Rosary, and my wife, Beth, prayed as well, but we had very little prayer together. And I think if anything transformed us as a family through Medjugorje, it was the emphasis on the need to pray together. Our family prayer prayed together has become the heart and soul of our peace at home. Again, as Ivan said this last summer regarding the primacy of family prayer: "Many people are concerned about forming prayer groups. The first prayer group should be the family. Then later you can have other prayer groups" (June 1990).

Specific Medjugorje Calls to Prayer

Let us examine the specific calls of prayer in the Medjugorje message, and then, under each category, see how these specific calls can be prudently and practically incorporated into today's family life.

The Blessed Mother is clearly calling for a greater generosity in both quality and quantity of prayer. As we examine the development of apparitions in light of Lourdes and Fatima in what today is called the Marian Age, at Medjugorje we see a completion of the gradual Marian call that asks for the greatest generosity in prayer. This is summarized by her expression "prayer from the heart." Heart biblically means the inner self, the core of the person. So she wants this prayer to be a loving conversation with God from the heart. And St. Teresa of Avila tells us that prayer should include two things: attention and devotion. We have to know to whom we're praying to, and we have to do it from the heart. There has to be love involved in this intimate act of mind and heart.

With this strong call to prayer, we also have to be reassured of what Our Lady said in this last message, that "your Mother will help you." If we truly make an effort to grow in greater generosity of prayer, then we've got to know that Mary's going to be interceding for greater graces to sustain us in our new efforts of generosity.

The Sevens

The Gospa began by requesting the daily praying of what are commonly known as the "Sevens." Seven Our Fathers, Hail Marys, Glory Bes, and the Creed. In the region of Medjugorje, the Sevens were prayed before Mary came, as a seven-point type of Franciscan prayer. Mary called for a reaffirmation of these Sevens to be prayed, but she added the Creed. It is particularly significant in our day that Mary is telling us to pray daily the Creed, because we have questioned and, further, we have doubted the most fundamental tenets of our faith. Where do we get the Creed? The Creed and the original Latin term "credo" means "I believe." And in the early Church when they used to baptize, especially with adult Baptism, they used to ask the question, "Do you believe in the Father?" And the answer would be "credo," I believe. "Do you believe in the Son, in the Holy Spirit, the Holy Catholic Church, the Communion of Saints?" "Credo, credo, yes, I believe all these things." Eventually what the Church did was to take a formula of what we believe and made it the Creed. So the Creed is really the love song of the Church. The Creed is that which attests to the one true Church in its fullness. Oftentimes we sort of hazily recite the Creed, but we should remember that there have been martyrs for almost every element of that Creed. So in this time of great doubt, Mary is saying to return to the practice of praying the Creed daily, return to what is essential to the faith. Throughout the Medjugorje message, we have a strongly sacramental and Catholic message. It's the message of the Gospel and the message of the sacramental life of the Church.

I'll never forget on a first pilgrimage to Medjugorje in December of 1984, I was staying with Marijana Vlasic who, with Jelena, receives inner locutions from the Blessed Virgin. I came downstairs one morning, and I heard this scampering upstairs (it was a two-storey place) and all of a sudden four little kids (I'm going to guess from about age nine down to three) came flying down the stairs in their jammies en route to the couch in front of a little family altar. A couple minutes later, Mom came down in her robe and they started praying in their native Croatian what I was later to recognize as the Sevens. In observing this scene, I noticed that there was not exactly perfect concentration by the children, there was squirming going on, and the older kids had a greater depth of concentration and participation than the younger ones. But I was so impressed that this was the first thing that they did before anything else on each and every day before meals, before showers, before even getting dressed. Before all else, that family started the day in prayer. And through a mere eight to ten minute investment, this family had done the most important thing possible in starting the day: invoking God's protection for that day. This practice remains very strong amidst families in Medjugorje. I would not underestimate the beauty and the practicality of families taking eight to ten minutes of the morning and coming together for the Sevens, because it does get the family praying together and it's just not too much of a time investment during the oftentimes frantic nature of morning time at home.

Rosary and Family Rosary

The Madonna has asked for the Rosary and the Family Rosary in a way so foundational, so central, so crucial to a true living of her message that I will devote the next chapter entirely to this most highly favored manner of Marian prayer and its inestimable graces for individuals and for families. The Rosary has been the single most prayer requested by the Blessed Mother, not just at Medjugorje, but in this whole age of Mary. If she is calling us to this prayer form with such persistence, then there must be special graces attached to its recitation, its meditation, in imitating Mary herself by pondering the Gospel life of Christ in our hearts. Let me just mention here what our Mother is basically calling for at Medjugorje regarding the Rosary. She started asking for the five decade Rosary daily, as she did by example at Lourdes and specifically at Fatima. Then, on August 14, 1984, she asked for the fifteen decade Rosary: "I ask people to pray with me these days. Pray all the more . . . Say every day at least one Rosary: Joyful, Sorrowful, and Glorious Mysteries.'' And as we'll mention in the next chapter, there's a particular beauty and practicality in breaking up the day by means of the Rosary, possibly starting the day with the Joyful, praying the Sorrowful Mysteries sometime in the middle of the day (oftentimes when we need that extra strength at mid-day), and ending with the Glorious Mysteries in the evening. We've got good examples in both Pope John XXIII, the ''good Pope'' who convened Vatican II, who daily prayed the fifteen decade Rosary; and Pope John Paul II, who likewise prays daily the fifteen decade Rosary in spite of a rather challenging schedule as the Vicar of Christ on earth.

Our Lady has repeatedly called families to pray the Family Rosary every evening, specifically for the conversion of sinners. And the importance of the Rosary (which again we'll discuss even more in the next chapter) is well captured in this June 1986 message, where Mary literally begs humanity to pray the Rosary with a firm commitment:

> Today I am begging you to pray the Rosary with lively faith; only in this way can I help you. Pray. I cannot help you because you do not want to be moved. Dear children, I am calling you to pray the Rosary. The Rosary should be your commitment prayed with joy. And so you will understand why I am visiting you for such a long time. I want to teach you to pray (June 12, 1985).

At least I know in my life, I don't think there was ever anything that I had to humble myself so low as to beg for. I don't mean in kidding with friends, in jest, but something that I wanted so badly that I truly begged for it. And when the Blessed Mother begs, we know she's not begging for her sake. Her begging bespeaks the importance of the spiritual sacrifices of prayer and penance that she's asking for, which we should keep in mind in our own efforts to incorporate her Rosary request.

As a summary of the importance of the Rosary, let me refer to the February 25, 1988 message, which gives us a flavor of the power of the Rosary prayer, especially in light of Satan, who is a reality we experience in the Church. Satan can be either de-emphasized to the point that he's not really anything except a cartoon character, or he can be over-emphasized to the extent that he's seen as the cause of everything including the stomachache after too much pizza and beer! In a sense, we can give Satan more credit than he deserves. Satan has to be seen in balance, especially in light of the ultimate victory of Our Lord and the final triumph of the Immaculate Heart. Nonetheless, he is real and is prowling like a roaring lion seeking the ruin of souls. Let's look at this February 1988 message:

> Dear children! Today again I am calling you to prayer and complete surrender to God. You know that I love you and am coming here out of love, so I could show you the path of peace and salvation for your souls. I want you to obey me and not permit Satan to seduce you. Dear children, Satan is very strong and, therefore, I ask you to dedicate your prayers to me so that those who are under his influence may be saved. Give witness by your life, sacrifice your lives for the salvation of the world. I am with you and I am grateful to you, but in heaven you shall receive the Father's reward which He has promised you. Therefore, little children, do not be afraid. If you pray, Satan cannot injure you even a little, because you are God's children and He is watching over you. Pray, and *let the Rosary always be in your hands as a sign to Satan that you belong to me.* Thank you for having responded to my call [emphasis added] (February 25, 1988).

The Rosary is a symbol of the special protection of Mary and the special role of Mary in spiritual protection against Satan. This role of Mary is referred to as early as the first book of the Old Testament, in Genesis, as foreshadowed in the battle between the Woman and the serpent. And St. Louis Marie de Montfort tells us that this is also going to be the final battle in preparation for Our Lord's second coming, the last battle between the Woman and the serpent. Mary in this message calls us to take the Rosary in hand as a sign of being on the side of the Woman, the New Eve, the new Spiritual Mother of the children of God.

The Greatest Prayer from God

The Blessed Virgin has given numerous and the most profound messages regarding the pre-eminent importance of Holy Mass. In this March 1984 message, she said:

> Children, I want Holy Mass to be the gift of the day for you. Go to it; long for it to begin, because Jesus Christ gives Himself to you during Mass. So live for this moment when you are purified. . . . If people assist at Mass in a half-hearted fashion, they will return with cold, empty hearts (March 27, 1984).

The Blessed Mother is saying she wants Holy Mass to be the gift of the day for the Faithful. But she also notes that the requirement, the presupposition for this gift, is a proper spiritual preparation. This is the old classical definition of what is called *ex opere operantis*, in other words, the subjective preparation for the sacrament. This basically tells us that the degree to which we are able to be united with Christ in the objective sacrament of Eucharist depends upon the degree of the individual's subjective spiritual state of preparation. The degree of reception depends on our personal spiritual predisposition for grace. In a full spiritual preparation, we are able to unite ourselves fully with Christ, receiving the fullness of grace in the sacrament of Eucharist. If there is a lack of full spiritual preparation, the degree of grace received is significantly diminished. And of course, lack of preparation can also regress to the degree of what is called "sacrilege." What is sacrilege? It is to treat something sacred in an unsacred manner. To try to receive our Eucharistic Lord in the state of serious sin not only prevents a reception of the grace of the sacrament, but it is also another serious sin. It is to say, "You, my Eucharistic Lord, are not important enough for me to cleanse my soul in preparation for You."

The principle of proper preparation for Eucharist must be considered in understanding Mary's comments concerning assisting at Mass in a half-hearted fashion. Again, scrupulosity should be avoided, for a lack of full preparation does not necessarily mean serious sin. But we should strive for the deepest spiritual preparation that's possible. The extent to which you prepare to receive Our Eucharistic Lord is the extent to which you receive the graces of that sacrament. She says along the same note in this May 1985 message: "Dear children, I am calling you to more attentive prayer and participation in the Mass. I wish you to experience God within yourselves during Mass" (May 16, 1985). So, what's the best preparation? Not only the fundamental requirement of being in sanctifying grace, but also our best possible spiritual readiness to receive Our Eucharistic Lord.

Another reference to the central role of Mass in the Christian life is found in this April 1986 message:

> I wish to call you to a living of the Holy Mass. There are many of you who have sensed the beauty of the Holy Mass, but there are also those who come unwillingly. I have chosen you, dear children, and Jesus gives you His graces in the Holy Mass. Therefore, consciously live the Holy Mass, let every coming to the Holy Mass be joyful. Come to it with love, and make the Mass your own (April 3, 1986).

This one message could be the subject of Christian meditation for years. How do we consciously live the Holy Mass? How do we incorporate the sacrifice of Christ to the Father by imitating Him in offering *our wills* and *our lives* to the Father also? The Mass is central. And that's why it reflects the sacramental summit of the universal Catholic Church.

What is the Mass?

What is the nature of Mass? And why is Mary so concerned with it as the heart of the Christian life? In this profound message, the Madonna speaks of the sublime nature of Mass:

> The Mass is the greatest prayer from God, and you will never understand the greatness of it. Therefore, you must be perfect and humble at Mass, and you must prepare for it.

The sacrifice of the Mass continues in an unbloody manner the sacrifice of Jesus Christ at Calvary. It is a real continuation of that one sacrifice. That means that what Jesus did on Calvary, sacramentally continues at every Mass. When the priest consecrates the bread and wine, transforming it into the Body and Blood of Christ, and he offers it to the Father, we are at Calvary — theologically and truly at Calvary. Oftentimes, we hear the comment that "Mass is boring, I don't get anything out of Mass." The usual response given in return is that we're supposed to go to Mass to give, not to receive, to offer God thanks for the gifts of the week. But even beyond this, we must remember that at Mass, it's not just our friends or family or fellow parishioners next to us, it's Mary at our left and John the beloved disciple at our right because we are sacramentally but truly at Calvary. And being at Calvary is not boring! It's the most profound thing we can experience in this life, being at the foot of the Cross where the graces for the salvation of all humanity, not to mention you *personally*, were merited by our Savior. This is the nature of the sacrifice of the Mass.

And what should our response to the sacrifice of the Mass be? First of all, as Vatican II calls it in the document on the Laity, we are to join the priest in offering Jesus to the Father. When he raises the consecrated Host, we are to give our *fiat* to that. We're to say, "Let it be done. I offer you to the Father with the priest; I offer Jesus to the Father for the salvation of the world for the forgiveness of sin." And in whatever words we want to use in the intention of our heart we are supposed to join the priest in his offering of the Eucharistic sacrifice. This exercises our priesthood of the laity in union with the ordained priest. Joining the ordained priest in his offering of Jesus to the Father at the consecration is the height of an authentic participation in the sacrifice of the Mass. And secondly, of course, we are supposed to imitate the sacrifice of Jesus by offering our own lives in union with Jesus to the Father.

Without an understanding of the sacrifice of the Mass, we can understand how people consider it boring, because they don't know the essence of what's going on up on that altar. That's why we have an altar. An altar is a place where we offer sacrifice. And what's a priest? By definition, a priest is one who offers the sacrifice for the people. And there is a victim; it's Jesus Christ. That's why Our Lady is saying, "I want Mass to be the center of your life." Because Mass brings Calvary to us, and there we have the graces of the redemption for all times. What flows from the side of Christ? The waters of Baptism and the blood of Eucharist which is the sacramental life of the Church. That is why Mary concentrates on Holy Mass so much, because she's trying to get us back to Calvary. The extent to which we don't want to get back to Calvary is the extent to which we're not going to get the graces that come from Calvary. It's absolutely crucial to her message and it's crucial in the teachings of the Church as well: the sacrifice of the Mass and our participation in that sacrifice.

Marija, during her talk to the pilgrims in June 1990, again reiterated that the Mass should be "the center of our life and it is the deepest encounter with God." She mentioned that we cannot exchange anything else for the Mass. Evidently, someone had questioned Marija about substituting some other act of charity with the Mass, some other good work. The Blessed Virgin evidently responded, "Go to Mass first, receive Jesus in this special way, and then the Holy Spirit will guide you to acts of love." So, if we're concerned about love of neighbor, get fed on the spiritual food of Eucharist and let the Holy Spirit come in to sanctify and guide us in our love of neighbor. This manifests the heart of Christian charity: love of God and love of neighbor out of love of God. We love our neighbor much better when we do it with Christ than if we do it without Him. Marija's comments about the Mass being the center of our spiritual lives is reflected in Chapter 6 of St. John's Gospel. Our Lord says: "He who eats my flesh and drinks my blood, abides in Me and I in Him" (Jn 6:54). Now there is no greater possible union with anybody than if we are in him and he is in us. To abide means to "dwell in," to "inhabit." It's clear enough how Jesus is in us when we receive Eucharist because we've received Him in His body, blood, soul and divinity. But how are we in Jesus? How do we "abide in Him"? Because when we receive Him sacramentally we become in a new and greater way in His Body, the Church. He's in us and we are transformed by the grace of Eucharist into a greater member of the Body of Christ. That's why it must be the center of our life. Vatican II says the Eucharist is the font and the summit of the spiritual life. It's the Alpha and the Omega, it's the beginning and the end. It's the source and it's the highest point of our spiritual life. That's how foundational this call of Eucharist is and this call of Holy Mass, and why Marija reiterates that the Madonna would like everyone to go to Mass daily if possible. She doesn't say it as a mandate, but as an invitation whereby we can receive our "gift of the day."

Family Mass

Experiencing daily Mass as a family can have wonderful effects in family life. The effects of sanctity and unity of the family are accentuated when the family is able to attend Mass together on a daily basis. Again, that's up to circumstances and prudence in individual cases. I know one father (and in this regard it is, I think, one of the finest examples of exercising his role of being the priest, prophet and king of the family) who says his first duty to his family is to make sure every member of his family who has received First Holy Communion gets to daily Mass. That's his first responsibility, and after that the other necessities can be taken care of. In practice, this sometimes calls for a bit of juggling. Sometimes two go in the morning, three go at night; one goes in the morning, etc . . . It is a challenging goal at times, but one of great spiritual fruitfulness. So when it's possible, to the extent that it's possible, the ability of families to go to Mass together daily is an excellent goal.

Again, remember Mary's call to bring the very young to Mass. Mass is also the Sacred Meal, the meal of communal celebration where we receive Our Lord of the Passion, Death, and Resurrection. There's been a tragic error of some young married couples in their decision to stop going to Mass during those years when their children are young, because they don't want them to disrupt the Mass. But they are missing the Eucharistic banquet when they need it the most, when their kids are young, and when they especially need patience and spiritual fortification. When they have to respond with unconditional love to the "unintelligible goo-goos and gaa-gaas" is when they need the sacraments. It's in those early years that they really have to be the unconditional lover. Parents have to love regardless of what the children give back. I know of a parish priest whose motto is this: "If I don't hear the presence of children in my church, then my church is dead." That's a beautiful notion of welcoming children to the Eucharistic Banquet. As parents will testify, they are going through the greatest suffering when their kid begins to act up, and so at these times they need real support from the rest of the parish. At those embarrassing times, parents are really uniting themselves with the suffering Christ! Again, we must use prudence when it's so disruptive that the priest can't continue Mass, but in general we've got to give the benefit of the doubt to the family. Those little guys are members of the Body of Christ too! We've got to give the benefit to the little ones. Look at the example of our Pope; he so much loves the young. He's the first Pope to write an apostolic letter just to the youth because he knows that the future of the Church lies in our youth. The general rule ought to be to always bring the very young to Holy Mass and not to stop that special grace for parents and children alike.

Eucharistic Adoration

Eucharistic adoration is also strong in the message of Medjugorje. In a 1984 Thursday message the Blessed Mother said:

Adore continually the Most Holy Sacrament of the Altar.
I am always present when the Faithful are in adoration.
Then special graces are being received (March 15, 1984).

The Madonna is encouraging Eucharistic adoration today, which unfortunately in many parishes has decreased in popularity. I've even heard things like, "It's against the spirit of Vatican II," which is a theological absurdity. Vatican II strongly suggests Eucharistic adoration and the living Church, since that time has strongly encouraged Eucharistic adoration. In fact, our Holy Father, Pope John Paul II, has sustained Eucharistic adoration in St. Peter's Basilica and has started adoration in St. Mary Major, the largest and one of the oldest churches in the West dedicated to the Blessed Virgin. So, it is most contemporary and authentic to have Eucharistic adoration, and Mary also promises her presence along side the worshipping Faithful. Where her Son goes, she goes as well.

When families can participate in Eucharistic adoration, it is of a truly profound and great spiritual value. Again though, parents can sometimes be tempted to do an all night adoration at the parish and miss the "domestic vigil" that they should have kept at home with their younger children. The grace of the present moment is dictated firstly by our God-given state in life as parents.

Read the Bible

The Blessed Mother in two messages calls us to read the Bible daily as a family. She says on February 14, 1984: "Every family must pray family prayers and read the Bible." And on October 18, 1984 again we hear the message about placing the Bible in a central position: "I call on you to read the Bible every day in your homes and let it be in a visible place so as always to encourage you to read it and to pray." How do we incorporate this as a family? Let me suggest a few practical possibilities. We can read a short Scripture passage after the morning praying of the Sevens. One family I know reads the Mass readings of the day with the children before they go to Holy Mass. The kids have time to ask questions about the meaning of the readings and receive their own brief Bible study each day. There can be some really beautiful domestic teachings and discussions of the faith that come from a family discussion of daily Mass readings.

Other possibilities include reading some brief Scripture passage before dinner starts or even during the dinner. There are so many different possibilities. Here again, there is great freedom and flexibility. I would just say, by way of suggestion, that I think it's more important to read a shorter Scripture reading, even a couple of lines or even just one line sometimes, than to read a chapter or longer passages, because most children aren't up to concentrating and penetrating the profound, bottomless meanings of the words of Our Lord. Practically, we must be realistic about their attention span. It's very difficult for children to listen, especially if we're talking about young children, for an extended period of time. But I think they do enjoy, whether it be at the beginning of dinner or in the morning, or after the Sevens, hearing the always provocative words of the Holy Bible sometime during the day. This sort of imitates the Benedictine way of meditation. The monks of old originally said that meditation was like the cow chewing cud. Chew a little bit, then it's regurgitated and it's chewed more, then regurgitated and chewed more throughout the day. And in one sense (rather a graphic example maybe), we are called to do the same thing with the inspired word, by returning to a passage at times throughout the day. So we're really not doing any extended Scripture exegesis for the family, but more of a word from Sacred Scripture to ponder throughout the day.

Consecration To the Sacred Heart and the Immaculate Heart

One of Our Lady's final prayer requests is the call of Consecration to the Sacred Heart of Jesus and to the Immaculate Heart of Mary. This has been a strong message with increasing importance in the later apparitions. It calls for an understanding of the basic theology of consecration. I'm going to delay discussing it extensively here because it will be treated more adequately in the final chapter on *Peace in the Family*. The act of family consecration to Jesus through Mary is a crowning of authentic family abandonment and true family peace. Parents ought to realize that they're ultimately not the last ones in charge of family life, but in a responsible way they can bring Our Lord and the Blessed Mother as the pre-eminent guides and guardians in raising the family in holiness. The essence of family consecration or any consecration is a promise of love. Consecration to the Hearts of Jesus and Mary is a loving promise of self and family to Jesus through Mary. And the intention of the consecration is to allow Mary to help us live out our baptismal vows. As I will mention, there are basically two options: one is to try to be faithful to Christ on our own; the other is to try to do it with the assistance of the Blessed Virgin to whom God has given this spiritual prerogative to unite her first Child with all of her later children, which is what we are. So, it's a promise of love and self-gift. And it's an efficacious promise. It is like the need of married couples to say frequently "I love you." The wife may say to the husband, "Do you love me?" or "You haven't said 'I love you' for a long time." If the husband then responds, "Well I did say I loved you on our wedding day. Didn't you believe me then? Wasn't that enough?", then we have signs of a weakened love. Yes, the expression and commitment of love was made on the wedding day, but love, by nature, is fertile. There is something natural and positive about the fruition of a vibrant love that says "I love you" daily. That doesn't put in question the fact that I loved my spouse on the day of the marriage commitment, but it's something alive and strong in my heart, and so I want to say it again. And that's the nature of daily consecrating ourself and our family to the Sacred Heart of Jesus and the Immaculate Heart of Mary, of daily saying to Our Lord and our Mother Mary, "Today, I love you, I give myself to you, and I want you to use your full power of protection in keeping me and my family in the will of God and in the bosom of the Church this day."

Let me here read just one message about consecration to give an idea of its importance in the mind and heart of Our Lady:

> Dear children, my invitation that you live the messages which I am giving you is a daily one. Especially, little children, because I want to draw you closer to the Heart of Jesus. Therefore, little children, I am inviting you today to the prayer of consecration to Jesus, my dear Son, so that each of your hearts may be His. And then I am inviting you to the consecration to my Immaculate Heart. I want you to consecrate yourselves as persons, as families, and as parishes, so that all belongs to God through my hands (October 25, 1988).

As we can safely assume from the Blessed Mother, this message reflects a perfect theological understanding of consecration: all to God through the hands of Mary. And why through the hands of Mary? Because that's the way God came to us in the person of Jesus Christ. As St. Maximilian Kolbe says, we should respect that order willed by God. We should go back to Jesus through Mary because God willed that Jesus come to us through Mary. And that wasn't a divine happenstance. There was a divine purpose to it, and one we should respect.

Summary

It's clear enough that the Blessed Mother is calling us to a recommitment, to a new generosity in prayer, both personally and in the family.

Certainly, in discussing the specific prayer requests, parents can get strong feelings of being overwhelmed, almost to the point of despair. This is certainly not the intention of the Blessed Mother. We must return to the fact that Mary revealed her call to prayer gradually over a period of years. We, too, must incorporate the message gradually, returning to the three principles of 1) prudence according to our state in life; 2) committed consistency; and 3) generosity. Much of the overwhelming feeling passes as soon as we *begin*, however modestly, to live her message of family prayer in the home.

It's important that we don't understand these calls as just more external rules, as burdensome, arbitrary norms to follow, just more things we have to check off a domestic list. It is not an external call. The externals are a means to what we might call an *incarnational change* in the family. That means a change in the flesh and blood of our family life, not just arbitrary external rules, but means of interiorly transforming the family. It's something that when properly incorporated will change family relationships. For example, we are not called to consecrate our kids to Jesus and Mary, and then go on to ignore their needs for the rest of the day. Prayer and consecration with our children should lead to a greater concern for their needs throughout the day, a more loving care in terms of their affirmation, their day at school, their friendships with other children, etc. And they, for their part, should begin to improve in regards to respect for their parents, more patience with siblings, and the like. Mary's message will, however gradually, begin to sanctify the heart of daily family interaction.

Family prayer will have fruits. We must be realistic regarding the sacrifice this calls for but we should also be realistic about the fruits we can expect. Now our children are still going to have fallen natures. They're not going to become transformed immediately into little cherubs without ever so much as a thought of sin or disobedience. But the real presence of family peace will be recognizable. It is a real tangible peace that the Blessed Mother bestows on us in the name of Jesus.

We've talked about a gradual incorporation of the message,

and this according to our state in life, but also we should not see the message of Medjugorje as an idealistic impossibility for families. It's not impossible. Some families are able to live the special call of the Madonna in its fullness. I mention this because in terms of cautioning about doing "too much too soon" there arises the other danger of doing "too little too soon." What's the criterion? It's the prayerful discernment of parents using that ongoing sacrament of Matrimony, and it truly is an ongoing channel of grace. An ultimate discernment factor is the spiritual fruit seen in the family. After giving it some time, do we sense the spiritual benefit the family is receiving? We know sometimes that one cannot see the immediate fruits of an action, just as when we plant the seed in the garden we don't see the flower in merely a matter of days. These things take time. Just as it took us time to get into the vice of not praying regularly, it's also going to take time to get us into the virtue of routine family prayer and to experience the fruits of that prayer.

One pressing, practical note, which applies to all important things we really want to incorporate: parents need to sit down and set times for their respective routine for daily family prayer. To whatever extent families are able to incorporate Mary's call of prayer, there is the practical need to sit down and to schedule. And that should be done with realism. I would say it is better to do less prayer *consistently* than to do more inconsistently so as to provide an ongoing and reliable foundation for stability and growth. This must be determined by the parents, for no one knows their children like their parents. And God speaks to the heart of parents about their children like God speaks to no one else. That's part of the sacramentality of marriage also. So, realism is committing ourselves to what we can do, and also realizing it's not written in stone. We may find we're really capable of doing a little bit more. Or we may find we've taken on a little bit too much in terms of generosity, and we have to reduce our commitment a little bit. Instead of family fruits, we may find that we're just absolutely exhausted, and we're not necessarily any closer to Christ. That might be an indication that we've taken on too much too soon. We need to be flexible. But I think we must be fair to what the Blessed Virgin is asking and, of course, none of us has Mary's vantage point of why she's asking so strongly for generosity in prayer in our present historical situation, why she's asking us to be more and more generous. The Blessed Mother is asking, in fact, she's begging for generosity from individuals and from family members.

Let me close with the penetrating words of the Holy Father, Pope John Paul II, that well coincide with the Medjugorje call to family prayer. He in part quotes Pope Paul VI in his message to today's Christian family:

> By reason of their dignity and mission, Christian parents have the specific responsibility of educating their children in prayer, introducing them to gradual discovery of the mystery of God and to personal dialogue with Him . . . Let us again listen to the appeal made by Paul VI to parents: "Mothers, do you teach your children the Christian prayers? Do you prepare them in conjunction with the priests, for the sacraments that they receive when they are young: Confession, Communion, and Confirmation? Do you encourage them when they are sick to think of Christ suffering, to invoke the aid of the Blessed Virgin and the saints? Do you say the Family Rosary together? And you, fathers, do you pray with your children, with the whole domestic community, at least sometimes? Your example of honesty in thought and action, joined to some common prayer, is a lesson for life, an act of worship of singular value. In this way *you bring*

peace to your homes . . . '' [emphasis added] (*The Role of the Christian Family in the Modern World*, No. 60).

This is the very same goal of the message of Medjugorje for families: to bring a real, living, spiritual peace to the home; and the channel of the peace of Christ to the domestic Church is she who is the Queen of Peace.

Chapter 4

Rosary and the Family

Dear children! You have helped me along by your prayers to realize my plans. Keep on praying that my plan may be completely realized. I request the families of the parish to pray the Family Rosary. Thank you for having responded to my call (September 27, 1984).

The call to pray the Rosary is the principal form of prayer requested by the Blessed Mother, not only in the message of Medjugorje but in the overall Marian message to the modern world. I want to discuss this favored Marian prayer under three categories. First of all, I will discuss briefly the Rosary in this general Marian call to the modern world. Secondly, I will discuss a little bit of the origins, the history, and the nature of the Rosary. What is this prayer of the Rosary that Mary has called us to so regularly? Thirdly, and most importantly for our purposes, I want to show how these two come together in the crucial Marian call to pray the Family Rosary. This is especially true in reading some of the recent interviews of the visionaries. They present the Rosary, especially the family praying of the Rosary, right after the general call to prayer and fasting as the most efficacious means of repelling Satan and of nurturing spiritual growth. It is absolutely fundamental. Now what I'm going to suggest is that if there is any ability to incorporate the message of Medjugorje as families, and if one is not clear where to begin, then I would strongly suggest starting with the Family Rosary, a regular commitment to the evening Family Rosary. This is because no other single call (and again, it's not more efficacious than the objective call of Mass — we're presupposing the Sunday obligation of Mass) incorporates so much of what the Madonna is asking for in terms of families praying together *as families*.

Call to Rosary in the Marian Era

Let me trace a little bit of the persistent Marian call to pray the Rosary daily in what is called the Marian Era. Why is it called the Marian Era? Because the Blessed Mother will not stop calling the human family to return to the Gospel, especially in these past one hundred and fifty years or so.

Lourdes

Let's begin a brief summary with the Marian apparitions at Lourdes in 1858. Here in this little French mountain village to the one visionary, Bernadette Soubirous, Mary appeared under the title of the Immaculate Conception. What was the overall message of Lourdes in 1858? The overall message was prayer and penance to God for the conversion of sinners. There were very few recorded messages that "Aquero" (the French dialectical word that Bernadette uses for Mary which means literally, "that one") delivered at Lourdes. Our Lady began the call to pray the Rosary at Lourdes by example. We'll see how this example gets more explicit at Fatima and also at Medjugorje.

What can we say specifically about the Rosary from the apparitions at Lourdes? First of all, Aquero is always holding the Rosary beads in her hands during the apparitions and is in fact praying the Rosary. In one early apparition account, the Blessed Virgin's lips were moving silently while the Rosary beads were passing through the fingers. Bernadette reported that she received an inner impulse to reach into her pocket and get her Rosary beads and begin to pray. It's very clear in the account that it's an interior impulse that directs Bernadette to reach in her pocket for her Rosary. She responded to the interior call and began to pray. Also at Lourdes, Bernadette spiritually prepared for her later apparitions by the recitation of the Rosary. As we'll see, this pattern will continue through all three of the principal apparitions of this Marian Age.

The basic message of Lourdes is prayer and penance. Our Lady said a few times, "pray for the sinners" and "do penance for the sinners." But it is not a very developed message. It's very succinct and very much to the point. But implicitly we have the clear call of the Rosary, and it is significant that Mary began the call for us to pray the Rosary by her own example, then followed by the example of Bernadette and the townspeople.

Fatima

Now we move to another mountain town. We should note with any honest investigation of Marian apparitions that Mary likes mountain towns! Lourdes, Fatima, Medjugorje. This seems to be in some aspects a way to protect the integrity of the message. It seems that the more simple and less educated the conveyor, the better the chance of Mary getting *her* message across as opposed to having the thoughts of the human recipient interfere. To my knowledge there has never been an authentic private revelation given to a theologian. Why? Because the theologian would classify it, interpret it; it would be qualified according to St. Augustine and St. Thomas, and expounded upon, etc. And then it becomes our message, not hers. So Mary often picks those we would consider socially unsophisticated and even rudimentary in terms of education. We know that St. Bernadette did not pass her First Communion exam the first time she took it, which is not necessarily a sign of a lack of intelligence but a lack of schooling.

In 1917 at Fatima, the Blessed Mother comes to us under a

new title, Our Lady of the Rosary. The visionaries at Fatima, Lucia, Francisco, and Jacinta, had the daily practice of praying the Rosary. After praying the Rosary on that given day of May 13th, Our Lady appeared to them. In that first apparition, Mary gave the words that she would repeat several times over the course of the apparitions: "Pray the Rosary every day in order to obtain peace for the world." What we had at Lourdes implicitly, we now have explicitly at Fatima. Pray the Rosary every day for what intention? For the intention of peace. And again we're going to see even more development between a global call of peace at Fatima and specifying the interior peace of Christ from which global peace must come at Medjugorje. It's also interesting in terms of the power of the Rosary to note what Lucia asked the Virgin in that first apparition. The Blessed Mother had reported to Lucia that she and Jacinta would go to Heaven. Lucia then asked about Francisco? Mary answered: "Yes, Francisco, too, will go to Heaven, but first he will have to pray many Rosaries." This gives us an idea of the incredible efficacy of this Rosary prayer. The one spiritual instrument she specifically mentioned that would be necessary for Francisco's salvation was the Rosary.

In the second Fatima apparition on June 13, 1917, the Blessed Mother instructed the children to recite what is today known as the "Fatima prayer" to be prayed at the end of each decade of the Rosary. Many are not aware that the prayer, "O my Jesus, forgive us our sins, save us from the fires of Hell, lead all souls to Heaven, especially those who have most need of Your mercy" comes from Fatima. How appropriate is the theological meaning of this prayer petition that seeks to redirect all souls to Heaven, coupled with a prayer of intercession for those in the greatest need. It is said in the devotion to Divine Mercy that God reserves His greatest mercy for the greatest sinners. Sometimes this can cause us a little distress in the sense that most of us are not the greatest sinners. We all do our strong share of sinning without any question, but most of us are not the greatest sinners. Why do we miss out on Our Lord's greatest mercy? Because it's with the greatest sinners that we can see the exercise of God's greatest mercy. We can see His mercy expanding not just from the domain of the essence of human sin but to the epitome of human sin, which gives us a better idea of the infinite nature of the mercy of God. So, too, in the message of Fatima, we have the prayer to extend God's mercy to those in special need, in the greatest need of His infinite mercy, which Pope John Paul II infers is God's greatest attribute!

In the third Fatima apparition on July 13th, we have a very profound revelation. We have the vision of Hell (which has also taken place at Medjugorje to reaffirm the reality of Heaven, Hell and Purgatory as the three possible states of afterlife). The brief time we have on earth (and really it is brief compared to the eternal ramifications) is for choosing where we want to be eternally. It is comparable to this example. Let's say we have three minutes to choose where we want to be for the next twenty-four hours. We don't consider that much time, but we've got to make the choice, and it will determine the destiny for the rest of our day. This is comparable to our having sixty or seventy or eighty years on earth in which time we must make a choice that has an eternal ramification: Heaven or Hell. The relationship of sixty years to eternity doesn't compare to the relationship of three minutes to a day. That's how vital, how far-reaching the effects of our choices in this life are. So Mary's revelation of these realities is a confirmation of the results of our human freedom, for better or for worse.

After the vision of Hell, in the July apparition, we then had a prophecy that the Holy Father would suffer much. And it is no coincidence that on May 13th in 1981, on the anniversary of the first apparition of Fatima some 64 years later, the Holy Father, Pope John Paul II, was shot in St. Peter's Square at the Vatican. The Pope incidentally returned to Fatima after that shooting to give thanks to the Blessed Mother because he attributed his rescue from death to her intercession. Our Lady then said at this third apparition that if people do not begin to pray and cease offending God, there would be a second world war. This was a conditional world war that in fact took place because we did not comply with the call of the Blessed Mother and her petition for the daily Rosary. Our Lady then said: "Continue to say the Rosary every day in honor of Our Lady of the Rosary to obtain the peace of the world and the end of the war, *for she alone will be able to help*" [emphasis added]. And again, this gets to the heart of sound Catholic doctrine regarding the Virgin Mary. Mary has a preeminence in the order of intercession. No one can intercede like the Blessed Mother. Why? Because no one else gave, if you will, *carne*, to the Incarnation. No one else gave flesh to the "Word made flesh." Can you imagine the incredible union between Jesus and Mary even before the birth of Jesus? Mary gave her own flesh and blood to God in those nine months of gestation. It's like having the Eucharist in us uninterruptedly for nine months, but more! No one else, to use a classical theological formulation, had an "intrinsic relationship with the Hypostatic Union," an interior role in God, the Second Person of the Trinity, becoming man and redeeming the world. And so, appropriately, no one has the power of intercession like this woman. And this woman calls us to the Rosary in order to obtain peace for the world, a peace which we know the world itself cannot give. So, whereas in Lourdes we have the call to pray the Rosary by example, at Fatima it is a very explicit and, in fact, an emphatic call to pray the Rosary daily for peace in the world.

Medjugorje

Now, in our present age, under the title of Mary, Queen of Peace, we have what we might call the full flowering of this same Mother's call to the modern world to pray daily the Rosary at Medjugorje. Let me begin with the June 25th anniversary message of 1985 in which Our Lady in a very straightforward Marian manner said: "I invite you to call on everyone to pray the Rosary. With the Rosary you shall overcome all the adversities which Satan is trying to inflict on the Catholic Church." Mirjana on this same day asked the Blessed Mother, "What do you wish to say to the priests?" Mary responded: "All you priests pray the Rosary, give time to the Rosary."

In a very dramatic way, the Blessed Mother is posing this same Marian prayer, the Rosary, as a principal means not only of personal conversion, but also as protection against the attacks of Satan on the Church. We mentioned in the last chapter the possible extremes of either under-emphasis or over-emphasis regarding the activity of Satan today, but in clear balance there is no question that Satan exists and is presently attacking the Body of Christ. And Mary, as Mother of the Body of Christ, calls us to protect ourselves. In the Middle Ages, Mary was referred to as the "neck" of the Mystical Body of Christ. It is not very poetic, but it gives us a concrete idea of her role. She connects the Head with the Body in the order of grace. And that's why in St. Louis Marie de Montfort's writings, to which the Holy Father has called us to return today, we witness the ongoing battle between the greatest creature and the most heinous, between Mary and Satan, in a battle foreshadowed in Genesis from the beginning. It's going to be the Woman versus the serpent. And the Mother of the Body is telling us to protect ourselves with this Rosary prayer.

The power of the Rosary against Satan is also spoken of in this August 1985 message a few months later:

Dear children, today I call you to pray against Satan in a special way. Satan wants to work more, now that you know he is active. Dear children, put on your armor against Satan: with Rosaries in your hands, you will conquer (August 8, 1985).

Please note two insights from this message. First of all, the more we know of Satan and his cleverness the worse it is for Satan. The more we think of Satan as an unreal cartoon character, the better it is for Satan. Like Pope Pius XII's statement about the sin of this century, "The sin of this century is the loss of the sense of sin." If we don't know there is a battle, we're not going to be prepared for one. The more we know that there's a battle taking place the more Satan becomes active, because he knows that part of his ammunition is gone, that is, the ammunition of secrecy. And so Mary again calls us to the Rosary, our armor against Satan in today's battle against an active aggressor. With Rosaries in hand, we will conquer.

Then, in what I think is the climax of this whole Marian Age and in her Rosary call to the modern world, the Blessed Mother invites us to the full fifteen decade Rosary on August 14, 1984: "I ask people to pray with me these days. Pray all the more . . . Say every day at least one Rosary: Joyful, Sorrowful, and Glorious Mysteries." There's a certain appropriateness about going through the full fifteen decades each day. We all have joyful, sorrowful, and glorious moments in each day. And the more we can unite our experiences with the joy and the sorrow and the glory of Christ, the more we are transformed into Him. I think this is especially important with the Sorrowful Mysteries. The more we can see our sufferings in light of the Cross, and not only the epitome of His suffering on the Cross, but also the progress of His suffering — from the agony in the garden, to the scourging, to the crowning of thorns, and so on, the more we can accept our daily Calvary. St. Augustine has said there is no better way to grow in the spiritual life than to meditate daily on the Passion of Jesus Christ. Pondering the Passion of Jesus is also a standard foundation of the spirituality of St. Teresa of Avila, the Doctor of the Church on prayer.

And because the Christian has to maintain a spiritual balance, we notice there are two sets of mysteries that have to do with joy and happiness and one with sorrow. The Christian also must realize that it's a dying and resurrected Christ. And so we also must meditate on the glorious events of Christ's life. In our own age, with so much reason for discouragement, we have to remember we are on the winning team. Christ the King will return victoriously. Mary's Immaculate Heart will triumph, Our Lady says at Fatima. Sometimes in our own examination of the events surrounding us, we lose the element of hope, and that's not appropriate for the Christian to lose sight of. We know that the Lord has resurrected and that if we remain loyal to Him, we, too, will ultimately experience the final resurrection of the body on the last day. The last two Glorious Mysteries give us a little indication of what happens to us when we are true to the first thirteen mysteries: our own final resurrection of the body and our own winning of the heavenly crown. That's the beauty of praying the fifteen decades of the Rosary on a daily basis. It does help us with the rhythm of our own day to unite all daily experiences, whether joyful, sorrowful, or glorious, with those same Gospel experiences of Our Lord and our Spiritual Mother.

What, then, do we have in this Marian Era in terms of the recommendation of the Rosary by Mary? Lourdes by example, Fatima explicitly, and ultimately the very clear call of Medjugorje for the full fifteen decade Rosary. There's no mistaking what the Blessed Mother is calling for. And like a good, persistent Jewish mother who's concerned about her kids, she's not going to let us off the hook! A mother could stop if it were just for herself, but a mother can't stop when it's for the good of her children. That's why the Blessed Mother continues this crucial

Rosary call even to our very day — for the sake of us, her children.

History of the Rosary

What is the Rosary, and historically where do we get this profound prayer? Let me discuss this briefly, because I think the old Thomistic maxim pertains that the more we know the truth, the more our heart desires the good. The more we understand the richness of the Rosary in its origins and nature, the more we are disposed to praying the Rosary. So, let's take a brief glance into its history.

Traditionally, we trace the Rosary, in the form we know today, back to the twelfth century to the person of St. Dominic. Historically, it is not clear exactly what was given by the Blessed Mother to St. Dominic, but there remains an appropriate connection with Dominic and meditation on the Gospel mysteries (a connection referred to in several magisterial documents pertaining to the Rosary). What is known is that St. Dominic was called on to preach against the Albigensian heresy. One of the major tenets of the Albigensian heresy was that matter is evil. St. Dominic went into the midst of the Albigensian heresy preaching the essential mysteries of Christ in the Gospel which, by their nature, are incarnational. In other words, they are physical and material. Dominic preached that God became man, so Christ inseparably united himself to matter. And He lived with matter — it's called a human nature. And He died on the Cross with a body, and He resurrected bodily. So we can't consider matter to be evil and hold the tenets of the Faith. As Dominic preached very strongly on this against Albigensianism, he stressed the humanity of Christ as a means of revealing His divinity. So Dominic encouraged the people, especially during parish preaching, to meditate on the fundamental mysteries of Christ in the Gospel. And in some form this is the result of a revelation by the Blessed Mother to Dominic directing him to emphasize meditations on the Gospel life of Jesus Christ.

After the initial revelation of the Blessed Virgin to St. Dominic, we have a period of historical development from the twelfth to the sixteenth century in the structure of the Rosary. The Rosary started as what was called the "Layman's Psalter" where the laity recited one hundred and fifty "Pater Nosters" (Our Fathers) which modelled the one hundred and fifty Psalms in the Psalter that the monks prayed. Gradually, one hundred and fifty Hail Marys were substituted for the Our Fathers, and fifteen Our Fathers were placed to break up these one hundred and fifty Hail Marys into fifteen sets of ten which we call the decades. So, we have one Our Father, followed by ten Hail Marys. We also started with anywhere from fifty to one hundred and fifty mysteries per fifteen decade Rosary in the thirteenth and fourteenth century, in some cases having a mystery for each Hail Mary. Gradually, and for a rather practical reason (because people grew tired of carrying around the books necessary for recounting all the mysteries), the number was reduced from as many as one hundred and fifty down to fifteen. And so, the "Layman's Psalter," in the beginning of the fifteenth century, began to be called "Our Lady's Psalter." Finally in 1569, Pope St. Pius V, the great Pope of the Rosary, a Dominican Pope, officially approved what is our prayer usage and our form today, which is the fifteen mysteries, the Our Father, the ten Hail Marys, and the addition of the Glory Be at the end of each decade. Also by the sixteenth century, the second part of the Hail Mary was added. Previously in the thirteenth century when St. Thomas Aquinas did a commentary on the Hail Mary, there was only the first part concluding with the word "Jesus." The second part of the Hail Mary, an ecclesial prayer to the Mother of God for us sinners at the most important times, now and at the hour of death, was added by the time the final papal approval was granted in 1569.

We see historically then that the Rosary comes to us as a combination of grace and nature, beginning with a revelation from the Blessed Mother and then developing as it was prayed in the living Church.

Nature of the Rosary

What is the nature of the Rosary? The Rosary is a beautiful blend of vocal prayer and meditation centering on the greatest mysteries in the life of Our Lord Jesus and secondarily on the life of His Mother that leads us to incorporate these mysteries into our own lives. It is again an incarnational prayer. In other words, it's a prayer that incorporates both body and soul, and that's the value of the beads. Back in the days of the "Layman's Psalter" in the twelfth century, they gave the laity beads so they could count their one hundred and fifty prayers. There is an important physical part (and St. de Monfort stresses this in his discussion on the Rosary) in using the beads because the beads keep "matter at the disposition of the spirit." The beads keep the body concentrated on the subject that the soul is pondering. That's the purpose of the beads, to physically include the body in the prayer of the soul. The physical concreteness of the prayer helps with spiritual concentration.

Let me treat the nature of the Rosary under three aspects: the Rosary is a) scriptural, b) Christ-centered, and c) meditational.

Scriptural

The Rosary is essentially a scriptural prayer, and this is true not only in terms of the mysteries but also in terms of the prayers themselves. Pope Paul VI called the Rosary a "compendium of the Gospel." Why? Because the Rosary is the greatest summary of the most important elements of the life of Jesus and in the faith of the Church. It's a compendium, it's a history, it's a theological summary of the principal events in the life of Jesus Christ. We start with the Annunciation, the beginning of New Testament salvation history. When Mary said "yes" to the angel Gabriel, then the God-man came to be. And from the Annunciation we ponder Christ's life through the mysteries recorded in Scripture of the joyful, sorrowful, and glorious events up to the last Glorious Mystery of Mary's Coronation referred to in Revelation 12 with the Woman crowned with twelve stars. So the mysteries of meditation provide a profound, yet succinct summary of the most important points contained in the written Word of God.

Not only is each mystery scriptural, but the prayers of the Rosary are also essentially scriptural. The Our Father clearly enough is a revealed scriptural prayer of Our Lord. The first part of the Hail Mary is the combination of two scriptural responses from the Gospel of St. Luke. The first is the response of the angel Gabriel: "Hail, full of grace, the Lord is with you." Note in Scripture that the angel does not say "Hail, Mary;" rather, he uses the title "full of grace" as a name for Mary. And no other creature could ever be called "full of grace." The Saints have excelled in grace, but only the woman who's been immaculately conceived possesses the plenitude of grace. So, "Hail, full of grace, the Lord is with you" speaks of Mary's very nature in her Immaculate Conception. Then we have the greeting of Elizabeth: "Blessed are you among women, and blessed is the fruit of your womb." I once had a student who said, "I just can't get myself to pray the first part of the Hail Mary, I just don't feel comfortable, I can't get the words out." I asked the student, "Have you ever read the first chapter of the Gospel of St. Luke?" "Oh, yeah, I'm always reading Scripture" was the response. "Well, then you've done it," I retorted, "you've prayed the first part of the Hail Mary." It's a unity of those two scriptural greetings to the Mother of Jesus from the archangel Gabriel and St. Elizabeth. The only non-scriptural aspect of the first part of the Hail Mary is the addition of the word "Jesus." But certainly this addition would not be a great difficulty for the Christian.

The second part of the Hail Mary is an ecclesial prayer of the Church which says, "Holy Mary, Mother of God, pray for us sinners." When I was a young tyke in CCD classes, almost all of us ill-formed kids used to pray incorrectly, "Holy Mary, Mother of God, pray for *our* sinners," you know those other people who sin, we should pray for them. No, fundamental to the prayer is that we are praying for *ourselves as sinners*. It's a prayer for us who need this Mother so much and need the grace of her Son so much. It's the humble prayer of a sinner. If you're not a sinner, you don't want to pray the Hail Mary because you don't need the Divine Physician. When you think you don't need the Divine Physician, then you need Him most of all because you have lost the fundamental sense of sin. So it's a prayer of the sinner for grace both now, to incorporate daily the process of conversion on our present spiritual journey of faith, and at the hour of our death, when we make the final decision where we shall spend the rest of eternity, which is the destiny of every immortal soul. Both these aspects of the Hail Mary reflect scriptural truths. So, I think it can be said plainly and with great confidence that the entire Hail Mary is a scriptural prayer, in the sense of reflecting scriptural words and scriptural principles.

We then have the Glory Be in the Rosary prayer which is the Trinitarian prayer of praise. The prayer reflects the angels' praise of the Trinity, because the utmost responsibility of the angels is to praise God. (That's why we do our guardian angel a great favor by making Eucharistic visits, for then he can do what's true to his nature and true to his vocation at the same time — he can adore God and he can also watch after us!)

The Rosary is Christ-Centered

Secondly, the Rosary is a Christ-centered prayer. Both prayers and meditations alike are centered on the life of Jesus Christ. Again, thirteen of the fifteen mysteries are explicitly dedicated to the life of Christ. As for the last two mysteries, the Assumption and the Coronation, the former, Mary's bodily Assumption into Heaven, is the obvious effect of her Immaculate Conception. We remember that corruption of the body is an effect of sin. If we don't have original sin, we don't have corruption of the body. So, of course, at the end of her earthly life Our Lady would be assumed body and soul into Heaven. And this in some sense awaits us in the fact that after the final judgment, we have the resurrection of the body on the last day. And with the Coronation, we too will receive our heavenly crown when we win the race, as St. Paul tells us. So the last two mysteries are a foretaste of what awaits us in a sense when we are true to the first thirteen mysteries of Jesus Christ. And I think if anything would frustrate the very being of the Blessed Virgin Mary, it would be the tragic idea that prayers to Mary stop with her and never have a Christological end to them. That would be the greatest frustration for the Mother of God, because it would completely thwart the deepest intention of her heart and soul which is to unite us with her Son. And in that process, we are also to have a living relationship with her, but not as the final end. Jesus Christ is the Alpha and the Omega, the beginning and the end, in the focus of Our Lady and in the prayer of the Rosary.

The Rosary is Meditational

Thirdly, the Rosary is a prayer of Christian meditation. In the teachings of the Church on the nature of the Rosary, it is understood as both vocal prayer and meditational. The ideal model is the Blessed Virgin herself. Scripture tells us that Mary always pondered the "things of God" in her heart. What got by the others at the historical events of these mysteries, in terms of significance, did not get by Mary. They became food for her pondering of heart and mind. And that's also the approach we should have to the Rosary, to ponder the things of God in our minds and hearts. And that's why understood correctly, for people to say, "I'm bored with praying the Rosary," is to say, "I'm bored with meditating on the Gospel." We must remember that the Rosary is also to be an invitation to Gospel meditation. We can never say: "Well, I've read John's Gospel and I've understood everything Our Lord said and did, and I'm ready for something else to think about." The Gospels are absolutely bottomless. We can never absorb everything in the mysteries of the Gospel. And so, if we understand the Rosary as meditational, we know that we can't be fully quenched in its recitation. We can never say, "I completely understand Calvary, I've exhausted its consideration; can you give me some new mystery now?" No, no, we'll never understand its sublimity, its profundity. Remember what Our Blessed Mother said about Holy Mass, that the greatness of the Mass is such that we will never be able to comprehend it. And the Mass is the bringing to the present the mystery of Calvary. We simply can't understand it in its fullness. These mysteries of Our Lord deserve our endless pondering.

Christian Meditation

Let me offer the three classic steps that are found in any authentic form of Christian meditation. And I think this will give us a good idea of what we mean when we say the Rosary is meditational. These three steps are consideration, application, and resolution.

By consideration we mean simply to ponder or to consider

the mystery at hand. Here we have great flexibility. Some people have a very good visual imagination and so they can close their eyes and easily visit in a vivid way, for example, the scene at Nazareth for the event of the Annunciation. They close their eyes, they see the Blessed Mother, they see the angel coming down. They can see the surprise on the face of the Blessed Mother although there's peace. Other people are not as good with visual imagination and they prefer to get something theological or concrete from the message. Mary said "yes" to the will of God, even though it surprised her. Let's ponder the beauty and meaning of this, or the greeting of the angel, "Hail, full of grace." What does it mean to be "full of grace"? What does it mean to have the Lord with you like no one else has ever had the Lord with them? To be full of grace is to be immaculately conceived and never to have said "no" to God. What does that mean? And this Annunciation, this announcement of the archangel Gabriel is to begin the nine month presence of Christ in the womb of Mary, the greatest tabernacle of God. So, we have great freedom with how we consider each mystery, whether we want to consider the mystery more intellectually or more visually.

Secondly, with meditation we have application. Application basically answers the question, what does the mystery have to do with me? And this is a very important part of the prayer of Christian meditation. What does this supernatural truth have to do with me? Pope Pius XII addressed these words about the liturgical mysteries, but I think they likewise have a relevance to the Mysteries of the Rosary as well: "Far from being merely events of the past, these mysteries are ever present and active . . . they still influence us because each mystery brings its own special grace" (*Mediator Dei*, 1950, No. 165). So what special grace does the Annunciation bring us personally this day? St. Teresa of Avila warns of a possible danger in pondering the mysteries of God and not applying them to self. She means that we can get great consolation out of thinking of the things of God but then we can continue to lead our life apart from the challenge of incorporating it into our life, without applying it to ourself. Mary said "yes" to the will of God when it surprised her; how do *I respond* to the will of God when it surprises me today? We must apply these mysteries to our daily living of the faith.

And thirdly with meditation, we have resolution: some practical resolve to incorporate personally the truth of the mystery. This is going to differ individually depending on the fruit of the mystery and its application. Again using the First Joyful Mystery, we could say that I did not respond to the surprising manifestation of God's will to me today when it didn't fit into my neatly calculated plan. I had my day set out and yet God manifested Himself to me and I didn't like it and I didn't respond well. Tomorrow I'll seek to better imitate the Blessed Virgin by better receiving God's sometimes surprising will. I'll seek to make my schedule more docile and subordinate to His manifest schedule. So it can be any resolution, whether it be specific or something more general. But some way of resolving to allow the mystery to enter more deeply and concretely into our Christian life. Now this third part of meditation doesn't mean that every time you finish praying five decades of the Rosary you are going to have five new resolutions. All we're saying is to let the pondered supernatural truth in some way enter your life. Don't just suck the mystery of its beauty and value and then not incorporate it.

So, consideration, application, and resolution are the basic foundations for meditating on the Rosary mysteries. And I think we can see that since the Rosary is both vocal and meditational, we can never say that this Rosary prayer has nothing more for me. We can never stop pondering and imitating the life of Jesus Christ.

The question is sometimes raised, "How do we put together

these elements in praying the Rosary?'' It's nice to talk about different dimensions of prayer but in what practical way do we coordinate these elements in praying the Rosary? Let me quote the words of Maisie Ward on this very question: ''The beads are there for the sake of the prayers, and the prayers are there for the sake of the mysteries.'' The beads support the prayers, and the prayers lead us to the mysteries. Sometimes I like to think of it as praying through the prayers to the mysteries. Take, for example, the Third Sorrowful Mystery, the Crowning of Our Lord with Thorns. We start with the Our Father and Hail Mary and we don't necessarily take away the value of the prayer when we pray through those prayers to the mystery. In the mystery, we realize what it means for Christ to be humble. At any moment of the cruel crowning, Our Lord had the power to take away the very existence of the guards by simply saying, ''Cease to be. I'm God and yet you scoff at Me, be gone.'' Nevertheless the humility of the God-man during this humiliation leads Our Lord to accept it for our sake. And so, the praying of the prayers allows us to ponder the mystery or simply even to stop and ponder the meanings of the prayers themselves, and that's fine too. Sometimes, we prefer to ponder the meaning of the words ''forgive us our trespasses as we forgive those who trespass against us,'' realizing the condition for us to be forgiven is that of forgiving others. And that's a fine fruit of praying the Rosary.

That's why the rule of thumb with the Rosary is to let the structure of the Rosary serve you; *do not serve the structure to the detriment of prayer.* The structure of the Rosary is supposed to serve us in prayer which is to converse with Him who we know loves us. The Rosary has flexibility, not rigidity, unless we put in the rigidity. This can happen when, let's say, I've got half an hour to pray five decades, and I'm on the Third Mystery, and I sense a profound movement of grace beginning while meditating on this mystery. But I'm over-concerned with finishing the five decades in the time allotted, so I dismiss this graced movement of the soul and just move on to the next mystery. Here, I may be serving the structure instead of using the structure precisely to enkindle these graced movements of the soul. When Our Lord speaks in prayer, we should generally abandon the structure and follow the movement of grace Our Lord wants us to receive. Otherwise, we may be missing an opportunity of having God speak to our heart on any one of those individual mysteries. Or, conversely, God may not speak to us in any profound way in a daily praying of the Rosary, in which case we should prayerfully proceed through the mysteries. But the Rosary is an instrument that serves us and our prayer life and should not be seen as an end in itself.

So, in this process of praying the Rosary we have great flexibility regarding the time, the speed, and the way of praying individually. When we're talking about a group or family praying of the Rosary, it's helpful to have a little more uniformity. We can have Mom and Dad who want a little deeper meditation, so they really try to slow down the Family Rosary; and then we've got the kids who are more into vocal prayer wanting to really speed it up. Usually in the context of the Family Rosary or group Rosary, we've got to make the decisions based on the common good of all participants. Sometimes we have to compromise to a certain degree. But in our personal praying of the Rosary, we have complete freedom.

Family Rosary

Most importantly for our sake, let's discuss the Family Rosary. Let me begin with two messages, early messages in 1984, regarding the call to Family Rosary. Our Lady said in September of 1984: "I request the families of the parish to pray the Family Rosary" (September 24, 1984). And in October 1984 she says: "Let all the prayers you say in your home in the evenings be for the conversion of sinners because the world is in great sin. Every evening pray the Rosary" (October 8, 1984). So, the Madonna is calling all families to an evening praying of the Rosary, not just for sanctification of the family, but also for the sanctification of the world — we are being called to *sanctify the world one family at a time*. That's the humility of the process of domestic sanctification, one family at a time. The Blessed Mother is also calling for the evening Family Rosary for the sanctification of the entire Body of Christ. These are the spiritual sacrifices that Mary can take to Our Lord to bring more people into the Body of Christ and to purify the Body of Christ. There is a social dimension as well but, first and foremost, it's a spiritual dimension.

Now of all the specifics the Blessed Mother is requesting of families, I would like to suggest that families begin with the resolute commitment to pray the Family Rosary each evening for the conversion of sinners. I say this because she's calling families first of all to pray together, to pray *as families*. We ought to have a commitment to praying the Rosary as families, or in many cases a recommitment to praying the Rosary as families. In the humanness of running the domestic Church, we falter and often we miss a couple nights or even a couple weeks. Then we must imitate Our Lord in the Fourth Sorrowful Mystery, where Christ shows us how to get up after falling. He falls three times to show us not only the weight of the Cross, but He shows us how to get up.

Families have to get up and it's very possible and probable that most families are going to miss occasionally. At these times we must simply return to the practice of the Family Rosary. And returning to this practice, we get the "habitus," the virtue, the good habit that helps us to pray the Rosary committedly and consistently.

The Family Rosary practice incorporates Mary's preferred prayer throughout this Marian Era. But it's also a preferred prayer called for by the Magisterium of the Church in this century. Pope Pius X, at the beginning of our century, spoke of the tremendous graces received by families when they take time each day to "pray the beads together." Pope Pius XII in the 1950's says: "There is no surer means of calling down God's blessing upon the family . . . than the daily recitation of the Rosary" (*We have learned*, Letter to Cardinal Griffin, July 14, 1952). This is not private revelation. This is the official teaching authority of the Magisterium, she who teaches in the name of Christ. And our present Holy Father, Pope John Paul II, in his document on the Christian Family, quoting Paul VI again, designates the Family Rosary as a favored manner of domestic prayer:

> While respecting the freedom of the children of God, the Church has always proposed certain practices of piety to the faithful with particular solicitude and insistence. Among these should be mentioned the recitation of the Rosary. "We now desire, as a continuation of the thought of our predecessors, to recommend strongly the recitation of the Family Rosary. . . . there is no doubt that . . . the Rosary should be considered as one of the best and most efficacious prayers in common that the Christian family is invited to recite. We like to think, and sincerely hope, that the Rosary is a frequent and a favored manner of praying" (No. 61).

The interior flexibility of the Rosary makes it particularly beneficial to family prayer. The Family Rosary is one of the few prayer forms that has the flexibility that could at the same time allow for vocal prayer, meditation and even contemplation — and all this while praying the same prayer. Children can have vocal prayer; parents can have meditation; and grandparents can even have contemplation (basically because they're not responsible for the discipline of the children during the Family

Rosary!). Their minds can soar like eagles' wings, as John of the Cross says. How many prayers allow people, at different stages of spiritual maturity, to benefit completely from the same prayer form? So, it's an incredibly flexible prayer form that benefits all family members at all different spiritual levels.

Mary is begging for prayers not just for the family, but also for the world. But to paraphrase Mother Teresa of Calcutta: the peace in the world is being disrupted first and foremost in the family. And the Family Rosary is a remedy to mend that family disruption, and then to make it fruitful for the entire Body of Christ. That's why, appropriately, the Rosary can be seen in a sense as a spiritual fence around the family. But a fence in two senses. In the first sense, to safeguard the family and to sanctify it, but secondly, to sanctify for the sake of the greater Body. It has a social dimension which reaches out into the Mystical Body of Christ in general, beyond the fence of the individual family. When it's offered from the domestic Church to the Universal Church, you have the flowering of the fruits of family and that's the notion of sanctifying the world in the Church one family at a time. So, for all these reasons, Mary calls families to pray these beads of home sanctification.

Practical Suggestions for Praying the Evening Family Rosary

I would like to sum up with ten practical suggestions (and that's what they are — suggestions), for implementing the Family Rosary. Some of them I think are very obvious. But I'd like to just go through them by way of a reminder. These are suggestions and, as always, they are up to the prayerful discernment of the parents as to their effectiveness for their respective family. So, use them only to the extent that they serve in your daily praying of the Family Rosary.

First of all, I remind you that the Family Rosary is not a

monastic Rosary. It is not going to follow the rule of silence. Expect interruptions during the Family Rosary. It's part and parcel of any prayer form when children are involved. Interruptions vary from the changing of a diaper (hopefully during the Sorrowful Mysteries to give you greater strength), to disciplining (stopping the little chatter that's happening in the corner by those two family members who have sort of fallen off, not into contemplation, but into some distraction), to even an occasional question to Daddy or Mommy of "what does that mean?", or maybe to a pause initiated by the parent to help the children to understand the mystery under consideration. If children are fundamentally in the dark about the mystery, then they can't meditate, they can't ponder the element without some notion of what it is. So, without encouraging interruptions, we must be realistic about the nature of a Family Rosary. And I think this could also apply to things like posture. You can talk about an objective criterion such as kneeling which can be the best posture. But, I simply point out that the most important thing is that you're praying the Rosary from your heart in the family. For some members, kneeling may assist that process but, in general, the important thing is that the body serves the spirit. It's more important for them to be in a position that allows for prayer, and sometimes kneeling can be difficult for children. Sometimes the focus for families can leave the Gospel mystery and go to the mystery of whether or not I will make it through tonight's Rosary on my knees. Then you're not communicating with Him who you know loves you, you're communicating with the two knees who you know are giving you pain. And again I'm not speaking against the beauty of praying on the knees, I'm saying, make sure its a means. Sometimes having the family seated, or even lying down at times, can assist true prayer more than a uniform kneeling.

One wonderful way of stopping interruptions of the Family Rosary is to place the phone off the hook or to unplug it. Now some consider that a cardinal sin but even in terms of moral theology we can say that the phone, too, is only a means. And in light of the last chapter, if family prayers are the first priority, then that means even phone calls are no exception (short of prudence regarding emergencies). But as a recommendation, it's nice to have the phone off the hook or unplugged for Family Rosary time, since evenings are normally prime times for telephone calls.

Secondly, I suggest the use of candles on a family altar with sacred images and turning off all other lights during the Rosary. I think especially with smaller children, this takes away the whole domain of sensitive distraction, because they have two options, either to ponder the darkness or to look up at the altar embellished with candles and holy images. This can really assist in focusing the senses of the child toward the altar of prayer. There is also the benefit of children pondering, for example, the image of the Sacred Heart of Jesus and asking why there are thorns around His Heart. It's good for them to see and to ponder these images on our family altars as a beginning in their understanding of how to meditate on the mysteries of the Rosary later. Especially with little ones, it seems to help focus their concentration.

Thirdly, get the children actively involved by having them lead the decades. Again, this will depend upon the age, but it's important to allow them that opportunity to pray and to lead. Realize though that you'll get anything from a fairly articulate Hail Mary of a seven year old to a three year old's version where you get the words "Hail Mary" at the beginning and the word "Jesus" at the end, but everything in between is a mystery in itself! At the same time, these little ones are really praying. And I don't think it's just pietism to say that the prayers of young children have a special place in the Hearts of Jesus and Mary because they're so pure. Theirs is so often the prayer of a child to the "Abba," the prayer of the child to the Papa or the Daddy in Heaven. And I know, in my own case, when I'm going through a difficult time, I'll just ask my seven year old or my five year old or even my four year old to say just a Hail Mary, to say it from the heart for Daddy. And I have sensed the spiritual strength that comes from those prayers, the prayers of the little ones. Our Lord had a preference for the little ones. Even when the apostles were trying to keep them away, He retorted, "Let the little ones come to me" (Mt 20:14).

So, encourage the children to pray, and allow them to lead the decades. In many families if this is prayer by osmosis, if they're used to this from before they can remember, then when they come of age they'll be the ones to ask "When can I start leading my decade?" Sometimes you'll want to start by giving them only three or four Hail Marys or a half a decade, because it could take ten minutes or more to get a whole decade out. But they want to take their role in family prayer, and I think that's a very positive way of having them enter into the Family Rosary.

Fourthly, the idea of the parents offering a meditation at the beginning of each decade is good. Something short, something maybe describing the mystery and then some application. We're talking about something very simple. Here is an example for the Fourth Glorious Mystery, the Assumption of the Blessed Virgin: "Mary is assumed into Heaven because of her purity and her sinlessness. Mother Mary, help us to be pure and not to sin today." What we do here is to introduce our child ever so gently to the school of meditation. We enter them into the school of pondering the mystery and then applying the mystery to ourselves. So, some idea of offering the meditation at the beginning is helpful.

Fifthly, ask the children on occasion what intention they would like to pray for. This introduces them to the habit and the power of the prayer of petition. They get the idea that they can pray for things near to their heart and that it has a real effect. I should also warn parents to be prepared for any type of petition that may come out. Expect anything from a prayer for the cat that drowned next door, to a prayer for a person who had the flu two years ago, to a prayer of a child that his father's balding would stop and that he would start getting his hair back again! All kinds of theological mysteries pop out when they start offering their own petitions. But they're praying nonetheless, with their precious little hearts, and this sustains a belief in the power of prayer.

Sixthly, we have found beneficial the Medjugorje practice of singing a brief refrain at the end of each decade. For example at Medjugorje oftentimes after a Joyful Mystery they'll sing the refrain "O Come Let Us Adore Him," or after a Glorious Mystery the refrain "Ave, Ave, Ave, Maria." These are short refrains, but they help the children to be redirected and refocused to the prayer. You may remember that very early in the apparitions, the visionaries asked the Blessed Mother, "How do you want us to pray? Should we pray or sing?" And Mary responded, "Do both, sing and pray."

The seventh suggestion consists in an occasional praying of the Scriptural Rosary as a family. As many of you know, the Scriptural Rosary is a little booklet on the Rosary that has a verse from Scripture for each Hail Mary on the subject of the respective mystery. It takes a little more time, but on occasion it can help remind both children and parents of the scriptural content of the mystery, as well as help in the process of keeping our attention focused on the mysteries.

The eighth suggestion is again the practical necessity of setting a specified time for praying the Rosary together as a family. This is especially important when we're talking about coordinating so many different family schedules to be present together. A couple of tried and true times for praying the Family Rosary (although they certainly don't have to be the only times) are immediately after dinner or immediately before going to bed.

These are times when we usually have most all of the family members there. I know there are other things that can creep in and take the place of that prayer time, like sports schedules, homework, school events, etc. But there should, nevertheless, be the fundamental commitment to the designated time for evening Rosary by all family members, and especially the children.

Consistency of practice is my ninth suggestion. As I mentioned before, don't get discouraged if you miss a few evenings. Some parents despair after a few missed evenings and quit the practice entirely. We all know the weariness and humanness involved in running a domestic Church. Just return to the practice afresh with a new commitment, a new resolve of will regardless of how many times you falter. Sooner or later, the virtue (good habit) of Family Rosary will lock in and really help you to be consistent as a family. Sometimes if you don't remember, the children themselves will remind you. They'll ask, "Aren't we praying the Family Rosary?" Or "Aren't we going to do any prayer before we go to bed?" And we're not talking about immaculately conceived children here, we're talking about ordinary children who get that feeling inside, whether they like it or not, that it's time to pray; we're supposed to pray now and we're not praying.

A tenth and final note regards "reluctant" adolescents. This is a question that often comes up: "How do we deal with our teenagers who don't want to pray the Family Rosary? Do we force them? How much do we include them?" Again, the answer originates from the discerning, prayerful decision of the parents using the marriage sacrament. By way of suggestion, I think there should be the commitment by all family members to being present during the praying of the Family Rosary. Even if it's just a passive presence. Why? Because, first of all, they're in the atmosphere of prayer. And secondly, it could dispose them to participating later. Ivan was asked during my last trip to Medjugorje, "Should parents force their adolescents to pray?"

I think his personal response has merit. He said, "Patience and parental love are the vehicles, not force. Otherwise, it [prayer] will just be mechanical." The practical application of this principle is always ultimately up to the parents. But I think it is important to say that a commitment at least to being present when the family prays the Rosary should be respected and implemented as seriously as any other family responsibility, like being present at meals, attending Sunday Mass, doing chores, etc. If we get back to the discussion of domestic kenosis, it should be seen in general as part of every family member's sacrificial commitment to the family, for the common good of the family.

Summary

There are many possible reasons for not praying the Family Rosary. It's one of the realms of possibility that seems endless, because families are so pressured by so many other needs. Putting all those possible reasons together, I do not think that they can compare with one reason why we should pray the Rosary. And that is that the Blessed Virgin Mary herself is asking us personally to pray this prayer daily for ourselves and for the Body of Christ. Pope John Paul II called Mary in his last Marian encyclical, the "spokeswoman of her Son's will." And that means when Mary calls us to pray the Family Rosary, it is because Our Lord is personally calling us to pray the Family Rosary. Of all the specific family commitments requested at Medjugorje (apart from those already obliged by the Church), I think the Family Rosary is the first place to start. Commit yourselves to the Family Rosary. Make the added effort and the fruits shall be plentiful, truly manifested in the sense of a new-found spiritual family peace.

Let me end with the June 1986 message of the Blessed Virgin who begs us to commit ourselves to this prayer. She says:

Today I am begging you to pray the Rosary with lively faith; only this way can I help you. Pray. I cannot help you because you do not want to be moved. Dear children, I am calling you to pray the Rosary. The Rosary should be your commitment, prayed with joy. And so you will understand why I am visiting you for such a long time. I want to teach you to pray (June 12, 1986).

Let's obey as domestic Churches the call of the Mother of the Body of Christ, and the call of Mother Church as well, to daily pray the Family Rosary.

Chapter 5

Fasting and the Family

I wish to tell you, dear children, to renew living the messages I am giving you. Especially live the messages regarding fasting, because your fasting gives me joy, and by fasting you will attain the fulfillment of the whole plan which God is planning here at Medjugorje. Thank you for having responded to my call (September 26, 1985).

The Madonna tells us in this message that fasting is a foundation for bringing forth into full flowering the message of Medjugorje. Note also how fasting has an integral role in bringing about the whole plan of God at Medjugorje. In this chapter I would like to talk about three aspects of this call of fasting. First of all, the general Medjugorje call to fast by the Gospa. Secondly, the nature and profound fruits of fasting, with an emphasis on understanding fasting in a positive light. Too often we have a negative notion of fasting, much like the negative notion of the sacrament of Penance which we discussed earlier. This is a great injustice to the spiritual gift that fasting is to the seekers of Christian holiness. Thirdly, and most importantly, I'll treat how fasting can be incorporated into our lives in a personal and a family way, how we can prudentially, and in a way that sanctifies our family, incorporate this call to fasting.

General Medjugorje Call to Fasting

The Blessed Mother began in 1981 by asking for Friday as a day of strict fasting. Then in August of 1984 she added Wednesdays along with Fridays as days of strict fast. She said, as conveyed by the visionaries, to "Fast strictly on Wednesdays and Fridays." Our Lady asked that this call of fasting be heeded, especially by the people in the region, with a "firm will." The visionaries then asked the Blessed Virgin, "What is the best fast?" Mary responded, "A fast of bread and water." So the *best* way of fasting in responding to Mary's fasting requests is the fast of bread and water. I will talk about the particular beauty that comes with the bread and water fast when we get to our discussion of personal incorporation.

In a July 1982 message, in the second year of the apparitions, the Madonna referred to the forgotten value of fasting by Christians: "Christians have forgotten they can prevent war and even natural calamities by prayer and fasting." This corresponds well with what Our Lord says about fasting in Sacred Scripture. In Matthew 17, when the disciples came back after being unable to expel the demon from the possessed boy, they asked Our Lord why their efforts were futile. Our Lord responded firstly that they lacked faith, and secondly that "this kind does not leave but by prayer and fasting" (Mt 17:21). This bespeaks the spiritual power of prayer when united with fasting.

Prayer and fasting is the appropriate combination when you're talking about the created level of human beings. Angels don't fast because angels don't have material bodies. The material order doesn't fast because its members, i.e. animals, plants, rocks, don't have immortal souls. Only the being with body and soul as his essence, only the human person, is called to fasting.

In the beatitudes, Our Lord simply presumes the practice of fasting by His disciples. "And when you fast" — it's a presumption, He assumes that after the bridegroom is gone (and He's been gone for a good bit, about 2000 years) that we, His disciples, would fast. He says:

And when you fast, do not look dismal like the hypocrites
. . . for they disfigure their faces that their fasting may
be seen by men. Truly, I say to you, they have their
reward. But when you fast, anoint your head and wash
your face, that your fasting may not be seen by men
but by your Heavenly Father (Mt 6:6).

So, Our Lady is asking for Wednesday and Friday as days
of penance, and specifically fasting. Now why would the Virgin
be coming to us in the twentieth century with this new call to
Wednesday and Friday fasting? Historically and theologically,
it is in no sense a new call. In fact, it can be easily documented
that Wednesday and Friday were the designated fasting days
in the early Church. The *Didache* (the Greek term for the document called the "Teaching of the Twelve Apostles"), written
somewhere between 60 and 120 A.D., was basically the first
Christian manual on how to live the Christian life, written probably by the generation that followed the apostles. In the *Didache*,
it states in the eighth chapter: "Do not fast like the hypocrites
on Mondays and Thursdays, you [Christians] are to fast on
Wednesdays and Fridays" (*Didache* 8:1). "The hypocrites"
was a reference to the Pharisees, and what the early Christians
wanted to do was to separate their ascetical practices from the
practices of the Pharisees to make clear the difference they pro-
fessed in the full Christian faith. But the point is that Wednesday
and Friday fasting was the earliest fasting routine of the Church.
In accounts of the history of the early Christian martyrs, we
know that the martyrs were often granted a final meal before
their death and that frequently, if the final meal was offered
on Wednesday or Friday, they refused it because these were
days of Christian fast. Other early Christians at least fasted
until three o'clock, the hour of the Passion. So we see that
Wednesday and Friday are not new fast days but are, in fact,
the oldest traditional days of penance in the Church.

Why is Friday the principal day of Christian penance? For the simple reason that Friday is the day of the Passion, the day Our Lord takes the Cross and pays the price for our redemption. In fact, in Canon Law (I don't mean just in the old Code, but in the 1983 New Code), it states Christians are all obliged to do some form of penance on Friday. And it is interesting to note that many countries in the Catholic world still observe meatless Fridays. Now, what happened in the United States and some other countries was that the National Conference of Bishops allowed us to substitute something else as a penance if we didn't want to observe meatless Fridays. But we are still obliged to give up something or do some act of penance on Friday. How many Catholics in America do you know that have substituted some other penance on Fridays in the place of giving up meat? The majority of people have just let the practice of Friday fasting die. It's a bit inappropriate for us to say we follow the Guy with the Cross on His shoulder unless we have at least a sliver on our own shoulder. And the foremost day on which we show our discipleship of penance primordially is Friday.

What's the significance of fasting on Wednesday? This is not as clear historically. It might have been the day of the betrayal of Judas, but we do not have historical certainty. Traditionally, Wednesday has been a day attributed to devotion to St. Joseph, foster father of Jesus and foster father to the members of Jesus' Body as well. In any event these are the two Christian days of fast. And if we notice in the Church today, the two liturgical days where Christian fasting is mandatory are on Wednesday and Friday with Ash Wednesday and Good Friday.

So, Mary at Medjugorje is in no sense calling us to something new with the Wednesday and Friday fast. On the contrary, she is calling us *to return* to the more committed ascetical practices as observed in the early Church. One of the great beauties of the early Church was that there was no division between ''spirituality'' and the daily routine of living. It was one and the same thing. You lived the Christian life whether you were praying or feeding your children or working, or you simply were not living the Christian life. There was no notion of "spirituality" detached from any event of the day. And in that more committed ascetical practice, fasting on Wednesday and Friday was the basic penitential practice. So it's important for us to understand that the Medjugorje call to fast is in no sense new, but rather a return to a profoundly rooted practice of the ancient Catholic Church.

Condensed in a single expression our Mother is calling us to a generous *fasting with the heart*. We see this in a 1984 message:

> Dear children! Today I call you to begin fasting with the heart. There are many people who are fasting, but only because everyone is fasting. It is a custom that no one wants to stop. I ask the parish to fast out of gratitude because God has allowed me to stay this long in this parish. Dear children, fast and pray with the heart (September 20, 1984).

What does the Blessed Virgin mean by the expression "fasting with the heart"? Again I think it is similar to what St. Teresa said about prayer. To have true prayer we need at least two things, attention and devotion. Attention means that we know whom we are addressing and conversing with in the prayer; and secondly, devotion means that we are talking to the person with love. And I think both these things should be seen in the practice of fasting as well. First of all, we're fasting as a sacrifice directed to God through the intercession of the Blessed Mother, and secondly, the intention of the fast is a sacrificial act of love for God. It's a fasting from the heart. It does not necessarily gain merit for ourselves, for the Body of Christ, or for the holy souls in Purgatory, if we are reducing our food intake on

Wednesdays and Fridays for the intention of losing those un-
wanted pounds we've been carrying around for the last couple
of years! Yes, we're denying ourselves food but we're not fasting
from the heart with the proper intention. And as the Blessed
Mother has also said, we shouldn't fast just because we're surrounded by others who fast (although there are not too many
regions of the world where this would be a problem). So, I
think it's fair to say that fasting with attention and devotion
means a fast out of love for God and humanity at the beckoning
of the Virgin. As St. Peter says, we are to offer spiritual sacrifices
to the Father in the proper exercise of our priesthood of the
laity. Father Slavko Barbaric has referred to fasting as "prayer
through the body."

Nature and Fruits of Fasting

Let's examine the nature of fasting and again, the positive
dimension of fasting. In general, Christian penance is any form
of physical or spiritual self-denial for the good of Christ, for
the good of the Church and for our personal purification. Fasting
is a major constituent of penance. So, normally fasting is going
to mean some type of physical denial in terms of food and
drink. Although, as we'll see in the message, the Blessed Mother
also calls us to fast in ways other than just food and drink,
including the areas of pleasure, personal preference, etc. But
fundamentally it's a denial of food and drink.

Let us look at a quote of St. Augustine from a sermon on
fasting that well summarizes the positive fruits, the rich positive
effects of fasting:

> Fasting cleanses the soul, raises the mind, subjects one's
> flesh to the spirit, renders the heart contrite and humble,
> scatters the clouds of concupiscence, quenches the fire

of lust, kindles the true light of chastity . . . Fasting loves not many words, deems wealth superfluous, scorns pride, commends humility, helps man perceive what is frail and paltry (*Sermons on Fasting*, II, II #147).

That is a penetrating summary of the fruits of fasting. I would like to discuss under three categories the sublime fruits of fasting.

A New Self-Mastery of the Body

First of all, we say that fasting offers us a new *self-mastery concerning the body*. St. Thomas Aquinas said that fasting is the "guardian of chastity." He specifically talks about fasting in assisting to remove lustful desires or the vice of impurity. In the positive context, we could say that fasting strengthens the Christian virtue of temperance. It grants us a new self-control in regards to chastity. This is a little known or presently discussed fruit of fasting.

Fasting has a direct effect on Christian temperance. Christian temperance is self-control regarding "taste" and "touch" with the help of God's grace. Taste deals with the domain of food and drink. Touch generally refers to the area of sexuality. Self-control in the area of sexuality is what we call "chastity." An interesting point that some theologians have made, and I think rightfully so, is that the more temperance we gain in the area of food and drink, the more temperance we gain in the area of sexuality, because temperance is the overall self-mastery concerning both these aspects of the body. Hence, a self-control with food and drink, something greatly assisted by the disciplined practice of fasting, can have a further positive effect in the self-control needed for Christian chastity.

I think especially in our own age, Christian chastity has likewise been given a negative connotation. This negative idea that chastity is "not fun" has tragically been accepted by many adolescents, by the middle aged, and even by some elderly. It's simply no fun to be chaste. Quite the contrary, it's no fun not to be chaste. It's no fun to be without the self-control needed to show love to another by respecting him in person and in body and to be without the physical control to respect your loved one both by what you do and by what you refrain from doing.

In the book *Love and Responsibility* written by Pope John Paul II long before he was pope, the Holy Father discusses what he calls the "true meaning of chastity." Chastity, he says, is not just a long list of "nos;" chastity is one great "yes," of which many "nos" are the consequence. The "yes" is to the truth that I am too valuable a person as an image of God Himself to be used by anyone else as a means to an end. I'm too valuable to be used as a sexual object. And that's a "yes." Because that's a "yes," there are some "nos" that I have to say to protect that "yes." I have to say "no" to pre-marital sex. I have to say "no" to adultery. I have to say "no" to homosexuality, to self-abuse, to contraception, to all the areas of sexuality that do harm to the dignity and the sanctification of the person. That's the yes and no of Christian chastity.

So, fasting is one of the greatest helps in acquiring and sustaining the virtue of chastity, that self-mastery of the body. Fr. Rupcic, a Franciscan priest from the area of Medjugorje, has said the following about fasting:

> It [fasting] is a simple means which allows man to show, to strengthen, and to stabilize his self-control. Fasting is the guarantee of his surrender to God in time and sincere faith. As long as man is not yet master of himself (of his senses), he will be unable to place himself completely in the hands of God (*Fasting*, pg. 24).

And this quote by Fr. Slavko Barbaric bespeaks the true freedom that comes from fasting. He says:

It [fasting] is a process by which we become free from and independent of all material things. And as we free ourselves from things outside of ourselves, we also free ourselves from the passions within us that are keeping our interior life in chains. This new freedom will make room in our body for new values. Therefore, fasting liberates us from a certain bondage and sets us free to enjoy happiness . . . By fasting we detach our heart from the things that tie us to the affairs of this world. Fasting will lead us to a new freedom of heart and mind (*Fasting*, pg. 19).

So we see that chastity, one fruit of fasting, is a freedom. It's a greater freedom because it presupposes that the body is obedient to the mind and heart and not the other way around.

A Greater Raising of the Mind and Soul in Prayer

The second great fruit of fasting is contained in the words of St. Thomas Aquinas, when he says that fasting "allows the mind to rise more freely to the contemplation of heavenly things." In other words, we could say that fasting allows for a new detachment of the soul from material things which allows for the soaring of the soul to God in prayer. The reason fasting can allow a greater soaring to God is because it confirms a detachment from the material order. We find this example many times in the Old Testament where the prophets fasted to prepare to receive the wisdom of God. The prophet Daniel fasted for three weeks until he received the wisdom and understanding that he asked for from God (Dan 9). Fasting, we could say, tunes the spiritual antenna in the process of prayer to hearing and receiving God's word. And I think in our own experience we can see that when we fast, the little things that often nag us, the little things that often seem so important, don't seem nearly as important because *we're hungry*. This can lead to a greater experience of detachment from the world, an awareness of the lesser importance of the material order and the primacy of the spiritual order.

It is also true that we pray better when we fast, and we fast better when we pray. It's much more difficult to fast on a day when we're starving from lack of prayer. Prayer assists the process of fasting and it focuses the fasting on why we fast. It lifts the mind to God and the soul to God through the body.

Offering For the Remission of Sin

The third fruit of fasting comes through an offering of fasting for the remission of sin. There are at least two major effects of this valuable spiritual gift offered to God. It's a spiritual sacrifice. And we know it's a spiritual sacrifice because it is a concrete sacrifice very close to the heart (in fact, very close to the stomach). There's no question that we are imitating in a concrete way Christ who fasted for forty days.

First of all, we speak of this effect of fasting in terms of the "little b" body, in other words, ourselves, our own body. Fasting has the ability to offer reparation for our own sins, and we know just as we receive a penance after we receive the sacrament of Confession, there is still a justice factor to sin that calls for atonement even after the eternal punishment for sin has been forgiven. This is the notion of temporal punishment as held by the Church from the earliest times. There is great wisdom in seeing the remaining need for atoning for sin after the eternal punishment and guilt of sin has been removed, because free human acts will always retain an element of personal responsibility. This remaining justice factor to sin calls for our humble reparation, and fasting is one of the best forms of reparation we can offer to remit temporal punishment. In this sense our fasting is a precious and purifying spiritual sacrifice.

Further, fasting is a tremendous sacrifice for the "big B"

Body, for the Body of Christ, the Church. And this applies in several ways. First of all, our spiritual sacrifice of fasting cleanses us as members of the Body. As we mentioned before, the Church is a church of sinners. We all sin, and because we sin we need the Church. Because we sin, we need purification for the Body. This is where fasting can cleanse the Mystical Body as a whole.

Fasting also helps the Mystical Body by offering sacrifices for the holy souls in Purgatory. The reality of Purgatory is very strong in the Medjugorje message. In some recent interviews, it has become known that Vicka took on voluntary suffering for an extended period of time with the explicit intention of offering these sizable sufferings as a sacrifice for the souls in Purgatory who had no one else to pray for them. This happened after Mary granted the visionaries some type of vision or experience (similar, but not identical to what took place at Fatima with the vision of Hell) of the three after-life states, which included Purgatory. We know that no one goes from Purgatory to Hell; it is rather a process of continued purification in preparation for the eternal glory of Heaven. And the Blessed Mother evidently stressed to the visionaries the importance of family members praying for their deceased by name for special assistance and special consolation as they go through the final purification in Purgatory. C. S. Lewis said of Purgatory (although he himself was not a Catholic) that it was like washing your hands before the Eternal Banquet. The host would like you to do it and you would like to do it as well, even if some pain is involved. So, there is a need of sacrifices for the holy souls in Purgatory, and fasting here again can have a tremendous spiritual effect.

Moreover, the offering of fasting can allow people to enter the Mystical Body, to enter the fullness of the Catholic Faith. And remember that Mary has said many times in Medjugorje (and throughout this Marian Age) that she needs these sacrifices.

These sacrifices of fasting can assist in healing the sad divisions among Christians and lead us to Christian unity in the one Catholic fullness. The value of fasting can likewise be used by Mary to bring non-Christians into the one Church of Christ. For Mary is never an obstacle to true ecumenism; she is rather the Mother of Ecumenism, leading her scattered children back to the one true Body.

Our Lady is the intercessor that offers these sacrifices to God through the one Mediator, her Son Jesus. When she receives these sacrifices from us then she acts as a Mediatrix (a secondary and subordinate sharer in the one Mediator of Jesus) and thus assists in releasing the graces of redemption that Christ has already merited. Mary's role as Mediatrix of Graces has been referred to several times at Medjugorje and has been part of ordinary magisterial teaching since Pope Pius IX in the mid-nineteenth century. Pope John Paul II has referred to her as the "Mediatrix of Mercy," especially in preparation for the second coming of Christ. So, she needs our sacrifices, and she applies it to the Body in the various ways we've discussed. Again, fasting brings forth priceless spiritual effects for ourselves and for the Mystical Body.

We have been talking about the profound spiritual fruits of fasting, but it's interesting to note that many people today are fasting for non-religious reasons. They fast for the physical fruits — the natural purification of the toxins in the body produced by fasting. People are fasting strictly anywhere from one day a week, to a full week fast, and sometimes even longer, doing so only for the sake of the physical benefits to the body. Obviously this is not the primary goal in Medjugorje, but at the same time there is the added benefit of proper stewardship of the body through fasting. So, in summary, fasting leads to a growing self-mastery, it leads to a freeing of the soul for greater prayer and, thirdly, to the remission of sin through a true and a concrete spiritual sacrifice we offer through the body.

Personal Incorporation

This is where we really get down to brass tacks about personally incorporating what Mary is calling for in terms of fasting. Who is called to fast? In the message of Medjugorje, as confirmed by the visionaries and confirmed by the priests at St. James Parish, the call to fast is *for everyone*. The call of fasting is a call in virtue of our Baptism. This is confirmed in the words of Pope Paul VI in his document on fasting and abstinence where he says, "Every Christian by divine law is obliged to do penance" (*Apostolic Constitution on Fast and Abstinence*, 1966, pg. 11). Fasting should be an ordinary part of the Christian life.

Fasting has become particularly difficult in the Western World, not to the credit of the Western World. We are in an era where the way to be self-fulfilled or self-actualized is tragically misunderstood as self-indulgence. But we know that the Christian mystery is that in order to self-fulfill, we must self-deny. You can't be perfected as a person without the process of taking up the cross of self-denial. So, all are called to fast, albeit in different degrees. This includes the young, the middle-aged, the elderly, and even to some degree the sick, although they're not necessarily to fast physically. Let me cite the words of Marija in June 1990 with regards to fasting and the sick: "For those too sick to fast physically, they are to offer their suffering with joy and to fast from alcohol, smoking, or to renounce television" (June 26, 1990). So, the Blessed Mother is the wise pastor and the spiritual director who safeguards our Christian vocation, at the same time she's saying all can sacrifice something. And in discussing the many options in types of fasting no one can say, "I can't give up anything" on Wednesdays and Fridays in response to our Mother's beckoning. The prudential question is, "What do *I* give up?" The answer to this question has to be decided according to our state in life. All cannot fast in the same way because of the great diversity in our situations and states in life. But the call to fast is a universal call that all have the ability to respond to in some degree.

Let us look at some different ways of incorporating the Medjugorje call to fast into our lives. I want to begin with what the Blessed Virgin has identified as the "best" fast, the fast on bread and water. Now, in many cases, we must gradually attain this goal. In most cases, fasting on bread and water as a two day a week fast is something which should be implemented gradually, particularly for those who have not had any experience in fasting. Some people have been able to incorporate it immediately, but that is usually not the norm. If fasting is a new experience, then a staggered increase could be more effective. The consistent practice of fasting is one area, in my opinion, where Catholics are behind our separated brethren in Christ, particularly our fundamentalist brethren. Catholics in the last twenty-five years have not been true to the universal Catholic tradition of fasting and, hence, have been bereft of its fruits in our contemporary era.

The "Best Fast"

Although the bread and water fast is not for all, it is nonetheless a realistic and attainable goal for many, especially when we're talking about single adults and young adults, as verified by the fasting practice at Medjugorje. The bulk of the Wednesday and Friday bread and water fasting has been sustained by single people, anywhere from the ages of late adolescence to people in their early thirties. This age group seems to have given the greatest response in generosity to the call of fasting. But I'm not saying that it's exclusive to those ages either. So, although the full bread and water fast is not for everyone, it remains an attainable goal for many throughout the world. Many others can, at least to some degree, put into practice the bread and water fast on Wednesdays and Fridays.

What's the particular beauty of the bread and water fast? Why does Our Lady call it the best fast? I think its beauty is firstly revealed in the symbolism of bread and water. Bread is symbolic of the Eucharist and also of our dependence on God, like the manna in the desert in the Old Testament. And water is symbolic of purification and life, the kind we receive in Baptism. So, in a sense, the bread and water reflect the sacramental life of the Church that comes from the very side of Jesus Christ at Calvary, the waters of Baptism and the Blood of Eucharist. So, in a real sense, for those who are capable, it's like saying, "Today, I live on You alone Lord. Today You are my Bread and You are my Life." This is particularly true when we join the bread and water fast to Our Lady's invitation of daily receiving Eucharist as "the gift of the day for the Faithful." This thought is well-captured in this pithy statement by Father Slavko Barbaric: "By being too attached to the contents of our plate, we run the risk of losing sight of our primary nourishment in which God offers Himself in 'a very special way.'" We would further have to say that in terms of generosity of sacrifice, obviously the bread and water fast is the greatest objective sacrifice and thereby the greatest objective spiritual value. It is then little wonder why the Virgin refers to the bread and water fast as the "best fast."

A few notes about the bread and water fast from the medical side. These come from Dr. Henri Joyeux, a French doctor and researcher from the University of Montpelier, who has been a principal investigator both medically and scientifically of the visionaries and of the concurring phenomena at Medjugorje. He has medically suggested the following points regarding a consistent bread and water fast on Wednesdays and Fridays. In general, he states that anyone can in a healthy way undertake the bread and water fast who is past the age of puberty and fundamentally in sound health. He makes a cautionary note for the elderly, suggesting that they might want to consult their physician first. But he asserts that this fast is not something that generally threatens sound health.

Secondly, he affirms that those who fast on bread and water should drink plenty of water, and he suggests a quart and a half of water intake a day. Our tendency when we fast is to stop drinking, but on the contrary, if anything, we should increase our water or our fluid intake.

Thirdly, Dr. Joyeux advises fasting on a type of whole wheat or hearty type of bread. If you notice in Medjugorje the bread they fast on is hearty. I tried to interrogate them for the recipe and to steal the secret the last time I was over there but to no avail! The homemaker I spoke with said it must just be their hearty type of wheat. Even so, Joyeux does suggest using a more robust, more nourishing form of bread than just a bleached white bread, which is much less nutritious and, thereby, has less sustaining value.

Fourthly, he strongly cautions against pregnant women and nursing mothers doing any type of strict fasting. And here again is where we humble ourselves to our vocation first. Our God-given vocation is our fundamental channel for working out our salvation. These again are simply medical suggestions, but I think they possess sound common sense regarding the best fast.

Modified Forms of Fasting

The best fast put aside now, what are other modified ways of incorporating the fast on Wednesdays and Fridays? One helpful modification is the practice of adding some fruit to the bread and water fast. This is particularly helpful for anyone who has trouble with hypoglycemia (low blood sugar). While the water can keep the body fluids going and a hearty bread can keep up the nutrition, the fruit, which supplies fructose, keeps the sugar going to the brain. So, the addition of fruit or fruit juices can be very helpful.

Another possibility is to add some type of Lenten foods like vegetable soup, a lentil soup, or some other type of meatless soup at some point in the day that can supplement fasting. Another alternative is to eat only one meal on a fast day. This was also a practice in the early Church. St. Thomas Aquinas discussed this type of fasting, commenting that he thought the most appropriate time to eat that meal was at three o'clock in honor of the Passion, symbolic of suffering with Christ until that hour when his Passion was consummated. So, reducing to a meal a day on Wednesday and Friday is another way to fast.

A further practical option is to fast on bread and water until three o'clock in the afternoon and then when duties and responsibilities tire us, we can continue the rest of the day fasting only from meat and treats. This type of partial fasting provides for some experience of the bread and water fast, but then when the duties of our state in life begin to wear us down (like the Psalmist says, "The evening flower that withers and fades"), we eat. Yet another good example of a modified fast is the fasting practice that the Church prescribes on Ash Wednesday and Good Friday. This constitutes a fast of one full meatless meal and two other meatless meals that together don't equal the full meal. This balanced approach to a modified fast allows for a true sacrifice, but one which will rarely take away from our abilities to perform the duties in our state in life.

At earlier stages of fasting, different ways of beginning a routine of fasting could be anything from skipping one meal a day, to reducing quantities of food consumed in all our meals, to fasting from meat and sweets on these two days in order to begin the good habit of fasting. Also, we can practice a more general fasting from things like cigarettes, alcohol, any area of specific pleasure, or even things like gossip, and speaking about other people's shortcomings. But I think it's clear in the message that where possible there should be some denial of food and drink because this is the essence of true fasting. Where a physical fast is not possible, as Marija mentioned regarding the sick, then there is always something else that we can fast from.

I remember giving a Medjugorje talk back in 1985 in San Francisco, and a woman who had to be in her late eighties or early nineties was trying to make her way up to the podium. She was handicapped and she could not climb the stairs to the podium, so I jumped off the podium and said, "Ma'am, did you have a question or something I could help you with?" And she responded: "I just wanted to ask you, do you think it's okay if I fast on bread and milk instead of bread and water?" Here was a poor elderly woman who could barely reach the podium, and in the very spirit of the widow's mite, asked if she could substitute milk for water. What humility and generosity.

What form of fasting should you personally incorporate? In one message, the Blessed Mother told us, "You all know what you can do." She is basically saying that it is up to our own prayerful and generous discernment. We all know what we can do. We also know what we can't do. Sometimes this will change as the circumstances of our lives change. But we can all fast to some degree and we should give the benefit of the doubt to generosity. We can always adjust down if we've sought to be too generous.

The spirit and consistency of fasting are important, but so too is the actual physical sacrifice. Fr. Laurentin in a penetrating comment on fasting discusses the proper relationship between the spirit of fasting and its foundation in physical self-denial:

> It is the spirit of the fast which matters, but one should not say that only the spirit matters. Our prayer and our spiritual experience reside in a body. They follow the

body's rhythms and are dependent upon it. *Depriving the body can awake the hunger of the soul* [emphasis added] (*Learning from Medjugorje*, p. 78).

So, while it is true that the proper spirit of fasting is essential, there is something likewise central about the denial of body to which all, excepting the sick and special cases, are called.

Family Incorporation

We've considered the general call, we've looked at the personal fruits, now we'll examine fasting for the family (and of course, the personal and the family incorporation are going to overlap to some degree). When we're talking about fasting as families, we have to go back to the first chapter and exercise the three principles on how and to what degree we are able to incorporate this message as families: prudence according to our state in life; committed consistency but with flexibility; and generosity.

To what extent can children fast? Fr. Slavko refers to the call to fast as a universal call, including children to some degree (depending of course on age). St. Thomas Aquinas in his treatment of fasting observes that children are not bound to the obligatory fasts of the Church because of their natural weakness, their need for nourishment owing to their rate of growth and their need to eat frequently and in smaller quantities (facts to which most mothers will readily attest — those constant little meals and little snacks!). So, the wisdom of the Church says children are not obliged to Church fasts, but St. Thomas also says it is important for children to begin to practice some fasting according to their age. And I think what he's referring to is the need to instill in the minds and hearts of our children the idea that Wednesday and Friday are *days of sacrifice for Jesus and His Body*. Our children should get the notion as they grow in the school of domestic spiritual formation that Wednesday and Friday are days that we give up something for Christ and for the Church.

Age will obviously play a major factor in what our children can prudentially and safely give up. Whereas it is possible for an older adolescent to try a bread and water (or bread and milk) fast or some other modified fasting options that we have discussed, this would not, in my opinion, be prudent for young children. And yet, as we shall now discuss, even very young children can make little sacrifices on these days as part of an overall family fasting effort. As children get older and especially as they enter later adolescence, there's a possibility of a greater and more committed fast. There should be a growing generosity with the growth in age. When they get the notion very early that Wednesday and Friday are days of sacrifice it only helps that gradual growth in generosity.

Practical Suggestions for Family Fasting

I'm going to suggest some specific areas, some possibilities where families can fast together (and in normal situations, the parents will of course be able to be more generous than the children). What are the areas in which we can start fasting as entire families on Wednesdays and Fridays?

First of all, let's begin with fasting from sweets — the "treatless" Wednesday and Friday. Again, it conveys the notion to our children that we have a spiritual and a social responsibility to the rest of the Body of Christ and on these days we offer up the candy or dessert. This is a good beginning of fasting for children (and in some cases adults as well), and it's something people of all ages can sacrifice.

Another family possibility is fasting from meat. This can have the positive dimension of bringing fish back into the diet. Fish is not only very good nutritionally but it has a beautiful

Christian symbolism. In the early days of Christianity, especially during the persecutions, when you walked up to someone you thought might be a Christian (and remember, if you made a mistake it meant your own martyrdom), you made a curved line in the dirt. If they were Christian, they took a stick or their own finger and made another curved line, touching your line at the beginning and crossing it at the end, which formed the image of the fish. And that was the sign that you had met a member of the Body of Christ. The fish was a symbol of Christ, a symbol of the death and the resurrection into which we're incorporated by the waters of Baptism. In many monastic traditions, fish is the major food. But apart from the sign value of fish, the meatless Wednesdays and Fridays do not hurt us nutritionally nor does it necessarily hurt the performance of our state in life, but it is a sacrifice. Sometimes it is the greatest sacrifice for Mom, who has the added challenge of planning the meatless meal twice a week. But that in itself can be part of the offering, and without jeopardizing the nutritional needs of our children, it constitutes a legitimate family fasting.

An area of family fasting that I strongly suggest, and one possible for every family, is a family fast from television on Wednesdays and Fridays. In one of the Lenten messages of 1986, the Blessed Mother said: "Turn off the television and renounce other things that are useless" (February 13, 1986). It must be said that, for the most part, the television shows watched by families certainly fall under the category of "the useless"! We are not saying that television is intrinsically evil but the vast majority of contemporary television programs are not only useless but directly harmful to family life and the proper faith atmosphere of the domestic Church. When television is renounced on these days and evenings, an amazing event can take place. On Wednesday and Friday evenings, we can begin the fascinating new experience of talking with the members of our family; we can share, read, play a family game together, and even pray together. It's an incredible new possibility. And to return to a previous comment: this is one of the greatest ages of "technological distraction" in the home. From morning to night, we can be distracted by some technological device: the walkman, stereo, Nintendo, television, radio, video player, etc. This is a danger unique to our age, and so we've got to be more sensitized to it. We must beware of being the passive receptors of electric things that do not necessarily enhance our spiritual life. It is true that the first couple of nights of this television fast may seem endlessly long because we have grown so accustomed to being entertained, but it can be a tremendously fruitful change in the long run. I think also for parents it would be a rather frightening notion to face God at the end of our lives and to have to say to Him that the reason we weren't praying the Family Rosary or we didn't have any real quality time together as a family was because we, as a family, were watching impure evening "soap operas" or violent police shows or some of the other T.V. shows that in no way respect or assist the sanctification of the domestic Church. So, I think fasting from television is a universal way by which most every family can begin the process of sacrifice on Wednesdays and Fridays.

And just in passing, to note a form of parental fasting that should be recognized as a legitimate spiritual offering is the oftentimes involuntary "fasting from sleep." This is especially true when we're talking about having infants or small children. This is pure penance. When you're getting up two and three times a night, that is a valuable spiritual penance that should be offered to Jesus through Mary. What makes an involuntary penance a valuable spiritual sacrifice, as opposed to what can become an occasion of sin, is how we respond by the intention of our will. If, as we get up the second or third time to change or feed the baby, we patiently endure this suffering and say, "I offer this for the glory of God and the conversion of sinners, for the holy souls in Purgatory, the end of the scourge of abortion, or for the child who's having a difficult time'' or for any other intention, then it becomes a real and valuable spiritual sacrifice. And it's an important sacrifice to offer, because sometimes this fasting from sleep can limit you from being more generous during that following day in your usual Wednesday and Friday sacrifice. So, don't hesitate to offer the fasting from sleep, a fairly regular form of fast especially with newborns and little ones.

One note on the flip side of this family fasting: It is important to have a balanced Christian approach in the family, so if you're going to sacrifice as a family, you had also better make sure to *celebrate as a family*. We as families should especially celebrate the liturgical year of the Church. And again, this takes time and it's got to be incorporated to the extent that it can be. But to celebrate the great feast days, to really celebrate Sundays and Holy Days, is an important balancing factor in family spirituality. Incorporate the children in these celebrations. Stop the usual protocol and have a cake on the great feasts, on the feast of the Ascension, on the Immaculate Conception, on All Saints Day. Have an All Saints Day party. Let the children dress up as saints and celebrate. We should do this, lest we give them an unbalanced notion of the Christian life. It's like the Rosary, two sets of Mysteries for the Joyful and Glorious and one set for the Sorrowful. We don't want to give the notion to our children that the Christian life is only sorrowful, all fast and no feast, that there's only a Passion and Death but there's never a Resurrection. Contrariwise, sometimes when there's an absence of fasting or penance, we could be giving them the idea that we're just a Resurrection people, and we're not a Passion and Death people, and that's equally dangerous. So, the balance should be in celebrating as a family the liturgical feasts as well as proper balance in family fasting.

As a final pastoral note regarding fasting and the family, remember that fasting is a means to holiness. Fasting is not an end in itself. Fasting is a means to sanctifying our families, and we have to avoid the danger of making fasting the goal instead of union of our families with Jesus Christ as the goal. And I think, for this reason if for no other, that Our Lord's great parable in Luke 18 of the Pharisee and the tax collector should be read and meditated on by any follower of Medjugorje. You remember the occasion when the Pharisee and the tax collector go to the Temple and the Pharisee states how he fasts twice a week and thanks God that he is not like the tax collector. The tax collector prays rather for God's forgiveness as a sinner. The scriptural passage ends with the words: "Whoever exalts himself shall be humbled, and whoever humbles himself shall be exalted" (Lk 18:14). I think this can be a valuable caution to the possible self-righteousness and pride that can come from fasting. It can become an occasion to look down on those who are not fasting even though, first of all, we have no ability to judge the heart, and secondly, we have no idea of the conditions as to why a certain individual may not be fasting. So we must strive to keep the proper humility that is part of an authentic Christian fasting from the heart.

We must further avoid the notion of fasting in the context of what I call the desire for a "spiritual trophy case." This is where our goal is to be able to boast fasting many days on bread and water. And I confess in my own case, especially in our early years regarding the Medjugorje fast, while living in Rome, that in the beginning months, fasting became for me to some degree an end in itself. The most important thing of the day was not my family responsibilities, but it was making it through the day on bread and water. This was true to such a point that at least on two occasions I remember telling my wife, "Beth, I'm going to bed because I'm so tired from the fasting. You take care of the children for the rest of the evening." So instead of eating a little something to get me through the evening hours and to tend to my first responsibility as Christian husband

and father, I deserted my vocation for the sake of the fast. This was a classic example of disordered fasting, because then the fasting hindered my God-given vocation in life rather than leading to its sanctification. Fasting became the end, and my family responsibilities became the means, instead of the other way around. This is inordinate: to see fasting as the spiritual trophy rather than a means of domestic sanctification.

The other extreme is to say that because I'm concerned about my family responsibilities I'm not going to try any fasting. In general this also lacks balance.

Fasting is a means and it's got to be seen always in terms of the sanctifying of our vocation. For those who feel called to a bread and water fast or a fast that continues into the later hours of the evening, it may be more prudent to eat a little something to sustain you in your family vocation. This is true especially when children are around, and you begin to become irritable or even to launch out in anger at the children. In this case, all you may be doing by fasting is offering reparation for your own newly committed sin against patience, and consequently there can be little net spiritual effect. So, the prayerful discernment of parents together, through the sacramentality of marriage, will grant the necessary family balance in this area of fasting in the family, combining the virtues of prudence, consistency, and generosity.

Summary

Of all that we have discussed in terms of implementing the Gospa's call to fast, the most important practical element is that in some small, humble way we as families actually *begin to fast*. We must prayerfully discern how, on this next Wednesday or Friday, we can begin to say "yes" to Our Lady's request of fasting as families. In some regards, I think it's even more important to get the entire family fasting consistently in a more modified manner than to have just one family member fasting more strictly. In this way we begin the virtue, the disposition of the will, in all our family members, to sacrifice for Jesus and for His Body through Mary, Mother of the Mystical Body. When we do this with a humble start, and perhaps with a more generous goal eventually in mind, then we can have the peace of knowing that we as a family are contributing to God's whole plan being fulfilled at Medjugorje, a plan with a consequence that will touch the nature and fiber of life throughout the entire world.

Chapter 6

Conversion and the Family

> Dear children, today I want to wrap you all in my mantle and lead you all along the way of conversion. Dear children, I beseech you, surrender to the Lord your entire past, all the evil that has accumulated in your hearts. I want each of you to be happy, but in sin nobody can be happy . . . (February 25, 1987).

The Blessed Mother reveals to us her call to wrap us in that immaculate mantle, that mantle that is stainless by its very nature. That's the meaning of the word "immaculata," that which is without sin. Also, as part of this process of conversion the Madonna calls us to let go of all the evil that has been accumulated in our hearts. She has asked for specific means of doing this because our sins, especially those of long past, can have a special tiring and laboring effect on the soul. And sin is the opponent of authentic human happiness, for human happiness is ultimately obtained through the presence of God in the heart. As St. Augustine says in the most famous quote from his book *Confessions*, "You have made us for Yourself, and our hearts are restless until they rest in You."

I would like to begin with the general message of conversion found in the Madonna's message. Further, I would like to treat the central means that she asks for in the process of conversion, the Sacrament of Reconciliation or Penance, which is integral in the Medjugorje call for a change of the heart. Thirdly, I will briefly consider the nature of sacramental Confession and the somewhat negative connotation that it has received in recent years and how theologically inaccurate this negative connotation is, because Confession is one of the only "no lose" situations we have in this life. And then we will discuss the incorporation of the message of conversion and reconciliation into family life. Of all the elements of the Medjugorje call to families, this is one that in a sense takes the least amount of time and can have the greatest efficacy for domestic conversion and for domestic holiness.

General Call to Conversion

The word "conversion," which comes from the Greek word "metanoia," means "a change of direction of the heart." In the Christian context, conversion means a changing of the heart away from sin and selfishness and to God and His family, the Church. I do not think it was accidental that at Medjugorje the apparitions began on June 24th, the feast of St. John the Baptist, considering that his Gospel call to "repent and believe" is an accurate summary of the Medjugorje message of conversion.

Repentance is a prerequisite for conversion. Conversion is something possible only when we have a clear understanding that we're going astray. We are not going to change our hearts unless we have clarity that our heart, to some degree, is pointed and moving in the wrong direction. This is why with the sacrament of Confession, an honest, humble examination of conscience is absolutely foundational to proper reception of the sacrament. Humility means "seeing ourselves as God sees us," no more and no less. It must be based on the truth about ourselves which is the only means by which we can turn our hearts to God: a response to the truth that to some degree we have our hearts directed towards things that are not pleasing to God. A heart cannot be changed without the conviction that it needs changing. Hence, repentance is foundational for conversion.

In this message of January 1988, the Blessed Virgin accentuates the need for a complete turning of our heart to God, and to seek God with a firm faith in the process of conversion:

> Dear children, today I am calling you to complete conversion, which is difficult for those who have not yet chosen God. I am calling you, dear children, to convert fully for God. God can give you everything that you seek from Him. But you seek God only when sicknesses, problems and difficulties come to you and you think that God is far from you and is not listening and does not hear your prayers. No, dear children, that is not the truth! When you are far from God, you cannot receive graces because you do not seek Him with a firm faith. Day by day I am praying for you and I want to draw you ever closer to God, but I cannot if you don't want it. Therefore, dear children, put your life in God's hands. I bless you all (January 25, 1988).

This is a message pregnant with many elements worthy of our pondering. It is a call to full conversion. This should tell us from the beginning that the process of turning our heart to God, although it may overcome many sins in the process, is a process that's never completed. As we have mentioned, it's like "the deer yearning for running streams." We should never say that our yearning for God can be completely satisfied in this life and that the process of conversion will at some time in this life stop. There should be a peace about our progress in the spiritual life, but never with the sense of a finality that the spiritual journey has been completed, that perfection has been arrived at because, should that sense come, then we have entered the state of spiritual stagnation. Like the nature of anything else that grows, if we say "it's done" and there's still by its nature the need to grow, then we do violence to this growing being. This is likewise true of the spiritual life. So, the Blessed

Mother calls us again to a full conversion to God, which is a lifetime process for the Christian.

Oftentimes we seek God only during problems and difficulties. The prayer of petition is a very important prayer but it should not be our only prayer. There's also adoration and thanksgiving and the prayer of reparation. So, in the process of the full conversion to God, a real spiritual maturity makes our relationship with God one that includes all these aspects, not just the prayer of request during difficult times.

Our Lady uses the notion of conversion as a prerequisite for our intimate union with Christ, the interior union with Christ which must be the goal of every Christian. We are reminded in Canon Law that we are obliged to seek Christian holiness. Holiness is not just for the few, but a universal call for the Body of Christ. All of us are obliged to seek what Vatican II calls that "perfection of love." Therefore, we are obliged always to seek conversion, the path to the fullness of love. In the midst of prayer and the confidence that comes with being in sanctifying grace, we can grow towards perfection, but never concluding that the spiritual process of salvation and sanctification is over. We cannot claim from an isolated event that happened in the past alone that "I am saved." A priest was once asked by a fellow shopper in a grocery store, "Are you saved, Father?" And Father responded, "Yes, I'm saved, we are all saved; the question is 'Will I make it to eternal life?' " We can say that Christ paid the price for everyone's salvation on the Cross, and in that sense, say we are saved by the merits of Our Lord's redemption. But the question remains, who is going to personally accept the saving graces of Christ in order to attain salvation? To receive the grace necessary for salvation, we must continually respond to the dynamic and ongoing process of Christian conversion that sustains and keeps alive a one-time faith decision for Jesus Christ.

So, the goal of the Blessed Mother in Medjugorje is our conversion, both by her intercession (by her prayers) and in a real way by her visit itself. Her concrete presence in Medjugorje is the most visible manifestation of her intercession. Just the fact that she's appearing is testimony to her intercession for us. And the goal of her intercession is our reconciliation with God, a full conversion to God, one that everyone must continue to seek humbly on a daily basis.

In the Medjugorje message, what are the specific means of conversion? First of all, we would say that the means for this turning of the heart to God is greater faith, prayer, fasting and penance. Even scripturally we know that these are the means to produce the fruit of conversion. The more we pray the more we know God. The more we know Truth, the more we seek it. The more we know God, the more we desire Him, and this comes in communication with God in prayer. The more we sacrifice for God in the area of fasting and penance, the more we're united with Him in His life of sacrifice and in our own self-mastery of the body. But Our Lady does underline one principal central means of conversion, and that is sacramental Confession.

Monthly Confession

The Madonna calls us to sacramental Confession at least once a month. Now let me note that not so long ago, when you asked your local parish priest how often you should go to Confession, the usual answer was about once a month. This did not indicate, as we'll discuss, that you were in serious sin on a monthly basis but rather that you wanted to meet the healing Christ once a month. You wanted to get the positive dimension of healing and grace that alone comes from the sacrament.

The Blessed Virgin stated as early as the third day of the

apparitions, on June 26, 1981, that Confession is a central part of this Medjugorje message. She said, "Men must be reconciled with God and with one another. For this to happen, it is necessary to believe, to pray, to fast, and *to go to Confession*" [emphasis added]. So note that the sacrament of Confession has both an immediate ramification in our reconciliation with God, and it is also the principal means for reconciliation among ourselves. It's like the virtue of charity: love of God, and love of neighbor out of love of God. They must go together. And in both cases, our relationship with Christ must come first; that's the foundation. It's also the foundation for any viable social work in reaching out to our neighbor. For example, in interviewing Mother Teresa, a reporter said, "You know, Mother, I wouldn't do what you do for a million dollars." Mother Teresa looked back at him and said, "I wouldn't do it for five million." In other words, no amount of money could make her do what she's doing. She's obviously doing it because she sees Christ in these people. And that's the only type of spiritual foundation that allows our social dimension of love to continue and to flourish. Otherwise, works of charity can be tremendously frustrating and can sometimes lead to despair because there will always be more poor to feed. Hence, what is true about love of God being the foundation of love of neighbor is also true of reconciliation with God. If we seek human reconciliation without reconciliation with our God, we're going to have a bottomless, a foundationless structure for establishing human unity. Men must be reconciled with God first and then with one another for true reconciliation to happen.

Very early in the Medjugorje message the Blessed Mother asked the members of St. James Parish to receive the sacrament of Confession at least once a month, and this was immediately implemented by the people. And now everyone who visits Medjugorje can see the endless confessional lines — a primary sign of Medjugorje fruits. What a profound manifestation of Our Lady's true presence! Many a priest I've talked to said they believed in Medjugorje, not because of any miracles of nature that they saw, not because of the sun spinning or Rosaries turning a gold color, but because of the numerous Confessions which they heard there. People who have been out of the Church for twenty, thirty and even forty years made a dramatic metanoia of heart in the few days spent at Medjugorje. Those spiritual miracles were far more convincing from the perspective of priests than any physical or solar miracle they could have experienced.

The Blessed Mother has made specific reference to the grave need for the Sacrament of Reconciliation in the West. She called Confession "the medicine for the Church in the West," and she stated, "Whole regions of the Church would be healed if believers would go to Confession at least once a month." This constitutes a particular call for us since "the West" typically refers to Western Europe and to us in the United States. It's interesting that when our Holy Father visited the United States on his last trip (I believe it was during his final stop which was in Michigan) he said, "Your Communion lines are very long, but your Confession lines are very short." So, many of us are disposed to receiving the sacraments, but to receive the sacraments of *our choosing*, and in many cases without the proper preparation.

On March 24, 1985 Our Lady gave the call to return to the sacrament of Confession before the Feast of the Annunciation. She indicated how important this sacrament was in order to celebrate the Feast Day properly. She said:

> Dear children, today I wish to call you to Confession, even if you had Confession a few days ago. I wish you to experience my Feast Day within yourselves. You cannot, unless you give yourselves to God completely. And so I am calling you to reconciliation with God (March 25, 1985).

So here we see that Confession should not be limited to occasions of serious sin; rather Our Lady seems to be saying if you want a complete reception of this liturgical feast in your hearts there is, as a condition for a full reconciliation with God and for our total surrender to Him, the need for frequent Confession.

In one message to Jelena, the visionary who receives the inner locutions, the Blessed Virgin made reference to those who have little or no regard for the sacrament of Confession or its importance. She said the following in a 1983 message: "If Confession does not mean much to you, you will be converted only with difficulty" (November 7, 1983). She doesn't say it is impossible. But she is saying that without this sacrament instituted by Christ, it will happen only with difficulty. Conversion is difficult enough because of our frail humanity, especially in our own age. So why would we willfully and deliberately refuse this Christ-instituted means of forgiveness, one which is the greatest and easiest way of conferring the grace of reconciliation with God and with each other? And the Blessed Mother confirms that this metanoia is going to happen only with difficulty unless Confession means much to us, unless we understand the essence and the gift nature of this incredible sacrament. This leads us to what the Vicar of Christ, Pope John Paul II, has said so emphatically in his 1984 document *On Reconciliation and Penance*. In this magisterial document, he reiterates that the sacrament of Confession is still the *ordinary and regular means* of forgiveness of serious sins:

> The first conviction is that, for a Christian, *the Sacrament of Penance is the ordinary way* of obtaining forgiveness and remission of serious sins committed after Baptism . . . In the school of faith we learn that the same Savior desired and provided that the simple and precious Sacraments of faith would ordinarily be the effective means

through which His redemptive power passes and operates. It would therefore be foolish, as well as presumptuous, to wish arbitrarily to disregard the means for grace and salvation which the Lord has provided (No. 31 Part I).

Now that's a very strong magisterial statement. The Pope is referring to the position that says, "I prefer to go directly to God for forgiveness of sins." While we must never judge the intentions behind this statement, we must theologically judge the act. The Holy Father is saying that to choose to bypass the sacrament of Confession is a mistake that denies us the Christ-instituted means of forgiveness as safeguarded and protected for us by the Church. As soon as Our Lord paid the price for our sins on the Cross, what was the first thing He did after His Resurrection upon appearing to His Apostles? He breathed the Holy Spirit on them and gave them the power of the forgiveness of sins (Jn 20:22-23). Imagine His joy in having paid the price for the sins of all humanity and then in giving to His Apostles this channel of forgiveness. It is almost as if Our Lord were to say, see what price this channel of forgiveness has cost Me — here, use it generously to remove the universal shackles of sin. He gave the Apostles this power to forgive or to retain sins. So, it's a very efficacious and precious sacrament, and Pope John Paul II is saying that we must consider this sacrament the ordinary, the normative, the standard means of forgiveness of sins. We can deduce then that if we're forgiven of sins outside of the sacrament, it's extraordinary. It's possible, we know, but it is outside of the ordinary means that Our Lord Himself instituted the sacramental means which we know has been present and operative since the first century of the Church. The theological rule of thumb is that we're responsible for using the proper means of grace as instituted by Christ to the extent that we know them. If we sufficiently know of the sacrament and yet refuse to use it, there is serious culpability attached to such acts, because we're saying we prefer another means to receive the forgiveness of Christ than the means that God Himself wants us to use.

Nature of Sacramental Confession

Why does He want us to use this sacramental means of forgiveness? Let's examine the nature of sacramental Confession. Earlier I referred to the Gospel of John, Chapter 20, where Our Lord returned after the Resurrection, breathed on the Apostles and said: "Receive the Holy Spirit. If you forgive the sins of any, they are forgiven; if you retain the sins of any, they are retained" (Jn 20: 22-23). What is the possibility of a priest retaining sins? The only criterion for retaining sins is when there is some clear manifestation of an absence of true contrition for sin. The only way we bind the hands of God, and especially the God-man who paid this price for the forgiveness of sins, is through our free will which refuses to seek and accept the mercy of God because of a lack of sorrow for sins. This is the sin against the Holy Spirit that prevents the work of the Sanctifier in our lives.

St. Augustine once made reference to Confession as the "medicine box," because in Confession we meet the Divine Physician; we who are in need of spiritual mending or the bandaging of the spiritual wounds of sin, receive grace through the healing Christ. Who would not want to go to the medicine box? Fundamentally, those who do not consider themselves spiritually wounded. And the tragedy of it all is that those who do not sense the need for the medicine box, who do not sense the need for the Divine Physician, are those with the greatest spiritual sickness possible. It was Pius XII who so accurately said, "The sin of our century is the loss of the sense of sin." This loss is the omission most damaging to our spiritual life. When we lose the sense of sin, we lose the sense of the need for forgiveness of sin, the need for the Redeemer of sin, and obviously for the sacrament by which we're forgiven of sin. So, with the loss of the sense of sin these days, it should be no surprise that there is a decrease of those frequenting the medicine box and receiving the sacrament that cleanses us from sin. They go hand in hand.

There's the story of the down and out person sitting on the street bench, and a priest happened to sit next to him and after some hesitation, the poor man on the bench says to the priest, "You know Father, I'd like to become Catholic, I'd like to join the Church, but I'm a sinner." And the priest responded, "Come on in, for we are a Church of sinners!" Yes, our Church is a body of believers who do sin and do need the healing Christ frequently to cleanse and mend us from the stain and the brokenness due to sin. If you don't happen to sin, then you probably don't need to bother with the Divine Physician or His Church of sinners. Our Lord so clearly says in Scripture that He didn't come for the righteous, but for us, the sinners. And it is the sinner who offers the greatest litany of praise and thanksgiving for the sacrament of Confession.

The Reality of Sin

The teaching authority of the Church continues to affirm the nature of sin as an offense against Divine Law, a personal offense against Jesus Christ and against His Body, the Church. The Church continues to proclaim the reality of serious or mortal sins. The nature of mortal sin is seen in the Latin root of the word, "mors, mortis," which means death. The Church still teaches, as She always will, that a single action with certain criteria, can kill or break your relationship with Almighty God. A single, gravely sinful action can remove the presence of the

Holy Spirit and sanctifying grace from our souls, evoking spiritual death. The three criteria for serious or mortal sin are, first of all, what is called "grave matter," that is, a serious breaking of the commandments of God and the teachings of the Church. Secondly, there must be sufficient knowledge that the action is seriously offensive to God. And thirdly, that there must be full consent of the will; this means that we freely choose to commit this seriously disordered act in spite of knowing its gravity. When we have all three of these criteria in a human act (and all three must be present for mortal sin), then we break our salvific relationship with God and force the Holy Spirit to leave the presence of the soul. And again we must be very clear as to who is choosing to break the relationship. God does not voluntarily end the relationship; rather, it's we who say by this act that we no longer want the presence of the Spirit and the interior union with Jesus Christ. So, mortal sin is still real, and the remedy for returning the person who has committed mortal sin back to the life of grace and the indwelling of the Holy Spirit is through the infinite mercy of Jesus so powerfully packed in the sacrament of Reconciliation. Without the grace of Confession (or a final act of perfect contrition in cases of emergency), we experience the final tragedy of human existence, the agony of eternal separation from the love of the Abba, which we call Hell. Hell is God's sad confirmation of *our* choice to live forever outside of the love of the Trinity. But to be sure, it is our choice, our tragic issue of free will that the Father sadly grants. At Medjugorje our Blessed Mother speaks strongly about the nature of sin, the activity of Satan, and the possibility of Hell, as confirmed in the vision that she granted some of the visionaries.

There is also that level of sin which is called venial sin. This is the slighter sin that, while offensive to God, nonetheless only strains the relationship with God but does not break it. What's the danger of the venial sin? The danger is that it can dispose the soul to more serious sin. We know theologically that venial sin is not cumulative in itself. We can't put together a number of venial sins, smaller sins, and have it amount to a serious sin, unless there's a willed intent; for example, I plan to steal five hundred dollars but I plan to do it five dollars at a time: we can't loophole God. Short of that, there's no cumulative effect to venial sin, but it can prepare us, serve as a foundation leading us to serious sin. And that's the great fruit of frequent Confession: removing venial sin which prevents the disposition of the soul to serious sin.

Fruits of Frequent Confession

There are inestimable spiritual riches to the practice of frequent sacramental Confession. We reap the benefit of a personal encounter with the healing Christ who has paid dearly to distribute His graces of forgiveness to each one of us.

We have the removal of our sins, whether they be serious or whether they be slight. We receive the grace not only in general to live the Christian life, but specifically to assist us in avoiding the very sins we've committed. That's part of the sacramental grace of Confession, the particular help in avoiding those very sins we've confessed. That's Christ the personalist. He's personally concerned with your and my every sin, and so He personally gives us the strength in this sacrament to avoid those specific sins.

Frequent Confession is especially crucial in battling against habitual sin, the type of sin we repeat over and over again. It is very difficult to get out of the vicious circle of bad habit, because every time we commit the sin in question, it becomes a little easier to commit the same sin again. That's the nature of a vice, it disposes us to a pattern of evil action. The grace received in frequent Confession (especially when followed by the reception of Eucharist) can break that vicious circle of bad habit and can gradually dispose the soul to the virtue or good habit corresponding to the particular area of weakness.

Another danger that often accompanies habitual sin is the possibility of despair, the greatest spiritual evil. And with despair enters the domain of the sin against the Holy Spirit. The sin against the Holy Spirit, as the Pope has discussed in his encyclical on the Holy Spirit, is not just any individual or particular action. It's not just to blaspheme God. It's not abortion or rape or murder or incest or attempted suicide. It is the willed refusal to accept the mercy of God. And that's the only sin that prevents the Holy Spirit, the Sanctifier, from bringing the forgiveness of Christ to us. There is no particular species of sin that cannot be forgiven, only the sin that refuses the mercy of God. And that's why Pope John Paul II has specified that God's greatest attribute is His mercy. An accurate image of repented sin in relating to God's mercy is to see the twig (our sin) in the white waters of the roaring river (God's mercy). Our sin, like the twig, can only be finite. We don't have the "being," if you will, to commit an infinite sin, because we're finite beings. And so, our greatest evil cannot compare to the ocean of the infinite mercy of God and the infinite graces flowing from the Cross. And that's why Judas, in his final sin of pride, essentially said, "I've now committed a sin so serious that God Himself cannot forgive it." This statement fundamentally reveals a sin of pride in saying that I am so significant that one of my actions has the power to stretch beyond the limits of God's mercy. And that leads to the sin against the Holy Spirit, the sin of pride and despair blocking God's forgiveness. Not only is a particular act of blaspheming God forgivable for the repentant sinner, but so is the sin of betraying or even killing the God-man. Even this sacrilege, Our Lord shows us, is forgivable by the graces of Calvary.

As to the fruits of frequent Confession, Marija, in one of

her talks in June 1990 in Medjugorje, reiterated Mary's request for at least monthly Confession and she also said that the Blessed Mother mentioned to her the need for Confession whenever "something is heavy on our heart." I think it's fair to say that this doesn't necessarily refer to a mortal sin, but to a sin particularly painful to us. This, too, is the time for approaching the priest and receiving the sacrament of mercy.

Let me read a passage that's been often quoted concerning the value of frequent Confession. It is a statement of Pope Pius XII from a 1943 encyclical that talks about the fruits of frequent Confession, a practice introduced, as Pius XII comments, by the Holy Spirit. It also strongly warns against any belittling of the importance and the value of frequent Confession:

> The pious practice of frequent Confession, which was introduced into the Church by the inspiration of the Holy Spirit, should be earnestly advocated. By it, genuine self-knowledge is increased, Christian humility grows, bad habits are corrected, spiritual neglect and tepidity are resisted, the conscience is purified, the will strengthened, a salutary self-control is attained, and grace is increased in virtue of the sacrament itself. Let those, therefore, among the younger clergy who make light of or lessen esteem for frequent Confession realize that what they are doing is alien to the Spirit of Christ and disastrous for the Mystical Body of the Savior (*Mystici Corporis*, No. 88).

Pius XII puts forth an appropriately strong condemnation of belittling or underestimating the value of frequent Confession. And again, what may have been true of possibly just younger clergy in the time of Pius XII must now be universalized in a warning to us all, both priests and laity, not to make light of the value of frequent Confession, which Pope Pius XII warns is nothing short of "disastrous for the Mystical Body."

Amidst the litany of benefits mentioned by Pius XII, let me elaborate on the benefit of the growth of Christian humility. Humility is to see ourselves as God sees us, no more and no less. Humility, as a call to proper lowliness, comes from the Latin word "humus," which means the "ground." Humility is the only real foundation for spiritual conversion because then we're true about what we do positively as well as negatively, and that is part of an honest examination of conscience. We should also be honest about the fruits of our lives. It's not honest for Michelangelo to say, "I'm a terrible artist, I can't draw a straight line," or for the Olympic gold medalist to say, "Gosh, I've got no coordination, I'm sorry I don't have any athletic ability." That's not humility, and, in a sense, that false humility can lead us away from the areas in which we really need to convert. So, humility is absolutely foundational for authentic conversion as well as for a proper preparation in receiving the sacrament of Confession. St. Augustine once said that we need three virtues for growth in the spiritual life: humility, humility, and humility.

In instituting this sacrament, Our Lord knew about our fundamental need to tell someone else, some other flesh and blood person, our sins. This is a need that we see both theologically and sociologically. We see this need exhibited, for example, on death row where so many inmates need to make final confessions, whether it be sacramental or just a verbal confession to a fellow inmate. Unfortunately, it must be said that today oftentimes, instead of making the trip to Confession, we make the trip to the psychologist. And we must never confuse a spiritual malady with a psychological malady. They are different phenomena. Certainly they can overlap in some cases, but by their nature they're different phenomena. Carl Jung, a well-known psychologist, said once that if people used the sacrament of Confession properly, he would lose ninety percent of his clients! Instead of this sacramental means, people often go to an analyst.

We're not trying to shed ill light on the proper role of the psychologist, which is truly an important vocation, but it's not the same as the sacramental vocation of priesthood as the spiritual liberator of sin in the name of Christ. They've got to be separated because fundamentally they treat two different human faculties. One primarily heals the emotions while the other primarily heals the spiritual state of the soul. Hence, the proper remedy will depend on the malady. But both roles of healing illustrate the fundamental human need to tell someone else our problems, our failures, and our sins.

This is why fundamental to the sacrament of Confession, to Mary's call, and to the experience at Medjugorje, is the crucial mediation of the priesthood. St. Paul said in his Letter to the Corinthians that the Apostles were "ministers of Christ, dispensers of the mysteries of God"(I Cor 4:1). That is the role of the priest in this sacramental context, to dispense the mysteries of Christ. This is why when we confess to the priest, we are actually confessing to the healing Christ through the priest. The classic expressions for the priesthood are "alter Christus," the other Christ, or "persona Christi," the person of Christ. And that's the one to whom we confess. Also with the human mediation of the priest, we have the spiritual counsel to assist us to avoid the sin in the future.

Beyond these reasons, Christ gives us the human mediation of the priesthood because we have that crucial role not only to be reconciled with Christ but also to be *reconciled with His Body, the Church.* When we sin, we offend not only the Head of the Body but the Body itself. It hurts the Body when we sin. The priest is the official representative of the Body of Christ, so when we receive the sacrament of Reconciliation from a priest, we're saying "I'm sorry" to Our Lord and "I'm sorry" to His Body. The mediation of priesthood allows us to make the reconciliation to the full person of Christ which includes His Body. Just as when Christ spoke to Saul on his way to persecute the Christians, "Saul, why are you persecuting Me?" He didn't say, "Why are you persecuting the Christians?", he said, "Why are you persecuting Me?" because we are part of Jesus as we reside in His Body, the Church.

Let us take a mundane example from the world of sports by using an analogy of a football team. When the right offensive guard jumps offside, the referee penalizes the entire team, not just the individual player who committed the penalty. For the guard to ask the referee to penalize him alone with a five yard loss, and not penalize the rest of the squad would be an absurd request. Likewise, for the receiver who catches the touchdown pass to expect the six points credited solely to himself and not to his entire team is equally absurd. But sometimes this is our mistaken idea of sin within the team of the Mystical Body. When we sin, it not only effects God and us, but it hurts the entire Body of Christ. And, thereby, if we seek full reconciliation, it must be made not only to Jesus, but also to His Body, the Church. When we confess to the priest as opposed to seeking a direct route to God, we also are reconciled with His Body, the Church.

So the Blessed Virgin calls us to this sacrament, not only for the purpose of spiritual assistance by the way of counsel, not only to fulfill this human need to tell someone else our sins, but also for that full reconciliation with Christ and the Body for which the mediation of the priesthood is absolutely crucial. And in Medjugorje, especially in the last four or five years, there's been a tremendous flourishing of vocations to the priesthood both for the parish and for the world. After my speech at a conference recently in Irvine, California, a young man mentioned to me how he went to Medjugorje over the summer and in Confession received the suggestion from the priest, "Have you ever thought of priesthood?" And to make a long story short the young man has just entered a religious order. It is important that we remember and relay to our children that the priesthood and religious life are still the highest objective callings in the Church. Because it is the highest objective imitation of the life of Christ. Subjectively we are supposed to follow God's particular vocation for us and that's our way to sanctification. But it is important for us, especially in our families, to continue to teach and to preach about the highest objective calling, because a lack of vocations is symptomatic of a problem in family life. The root of vocations is the domestic Church and when the domestic Church is not trying to live a life of sanctification, we are not going to have the type of domestic atmosphere to allow the seed of a vocation to begin to grow in the hearts of our children. When there is an absence of vocations, we are making a clear statement about the shortcomings of contemporary family life and society as well. We can also be left without two inestimable spiritual gifts that the Madonna of Medjugorje is emphatically calling us to: the sacraments of Eucharist and Confession.

Preparation for Sacramental Confession

The Blessed Mother has warned against a type of mechanical reception of the sacrament of Penance, a Confession lacking proper preparation. She said in this message transmitted through Jelena: "Do not go to Confession from habit, to stay the same after it. No, that is not good. Confession should give drive to your faith. It should stir you and draw you near to Jesus" (November 9, 1983). How then concretely do we properly prepare for and receive the sacrament of Confession? Let us briefly mention by way of review the five basic steps for proper preparation and reception of the sacrament of Confession.

First, we have the examination of conscience. This is to examine our lives since our last Confession in light of the Ten Commandments, the teachings of the Church, and the general dictates of the Christian life. Again this should be an honest examination of our faults based on humility, which is founded on truth.

Secondly, we should enkindle an authentic contrition for our faults. What is contrition? Contrition is a sincere sorrow for having offended God, coupled with the firm resolution to avoid the sin in the future. The latter resolution is an absolute requirement for true contrition. As a young lad I was with a friend in front of the candy store on the corner where we were contemplating pilfering some candy under the category of cold, hard theft. As we were discussing the possible act of stealing candy, the friend, who was also Catholic, mentioned to me, "Well, all we have to do if we steal this candy is to go to Confession. Then we can come back and take some more candy, and then we can return to Confession, and we can continue taking candy as long as we go to Confession!" Clearly my young accomplice did not understand the second aspect of true contrition, which is the firm resolve to avoid the sin in the future. That does not necessarily mean, by the way, that if we do, through continued human weakness, commit the sin again that we didn't really have the true contrition the first time. No, as long as there is an authentic commitment of the will to avoid the sin in the future, that is the necessary foundation for contrition.

How do we *enkindle* contrition? Simply by thinking of the sin and realizing that this action has hurt our all-loving Lord, it has hurt His Body, our brothers and sisters in Christ, and it has hurt ourselves. For sin frustrates our very being; sin prevents the fulfillment of human life; sin is cancerous to the human pursuit of happiness and the ultimate purpose of human existence which is eternal life with God. Sin can transform the human person into the boat that never sails, the car that never runs, the creature that never reaches that for which it was created. And naturally and even supernaturally we could say, when we truly ponder sin, we grieve over this vehicle of hurt for so many. Not in a morose way but in an authentic and a balanced way, we should experience the grief that accompanies true sorrow for sin.

Thirdly, we confess all sins to the priest. This is especially important in regards to serious sins. But, of course, the idea of Confession is to clean the spiritual slate, and again, at Medjugorje the incredible process of purification is so apparent. And it's not only one or two priests who have returned from Medjugorje and said, "I started my trip at Medjugorje by taking time in the confessional, and that's all I needed. When I heard these humble Confessions, I knew there had to be a special presence of Mary in this place." So it's a complete cleaning. The only thing that can prevent the interior cleaning is simply by not asking for forgiveness. One sign of an absence of contrition can be an unwillingness to actually confess the sin. While we cannot universalize this principle, it is in many cases, a sign of a lack of complete contrition for the sin.

All serious sins need to be specifically confessed. It's like locks on the door. If we have three locks on the door, and we unlock only two, the door is still kept from being opened because of the third lock. This is analogous to the nature of the serious sin. To confess only two of three mortal sins is still to prevent the return of the Holy Spirit to the soul because of that remaining serious offense against God's love. And this is true relationally as well. For example, if I were to go home to my wife and say, "Beth, I'm sorry because, firstly, I've committed adultery; secondly, I've stolen a thousand dollars from work; and thirdly, I've killed your mother. Now dear, I am sincerely sorry for the sins of adultery and grand theft but I really had to do your mother in. Can we be reconciled anyway, since I'm really sorry for the other two?" This would be a sadly confused expectation in the domain of human relations; similarly, it's a sadly confused expectation in our relationship with Almighty God. The only thing that limits the infinite mercy of God is our refusal to ask for it in the confessional. So, we must clean the entire slate by confessing all sins to the priest.

A major hesitancy in telling the priest all of our sins is the idea that our particular sins are really going to shock the priest. But I'll always remember the comment made to me by a priest who was a confessor (a priest who spends eight to ten hours a day in the confessional as his principal gift to the Church). This confessor said to me that the vast majority of people confess the same type of sins. At one point he said it can even get boring to hear confessions, not in the sense of dispensing the sacrament itself, but in the great redundancy of the type of sins that people confess. So, we should remove the temptations that can arise in the confessional line, when we think that, in comparison to everyone else's sins, our confession is going to be the "Jack-the-Ripper" confession, and the priest is going to be so shocked by our sins that his Roman collar is going to spin around his neck out of horror and fright! More often, that's our own misconception of our sins. And again, it can be an element of pride that places our sins in a competing position with God's infinite mercy and Jesus' great triumph over sin.

The fourth step in properly receiving Confession is to have the resolve, as we've already discussed, to avoid the sins in the future, a firm resolution of the will to avoid these specific sins just confessed. And fifthly, we have the performance of penance. Penance is a sacrificial act, whether in the form of prayer or an act of charity or some act of atonement, which shows both gratitude for forgiveness and is a sign of true contrition. So, it's important that we perform the penance assigned to us by the priest.

Moreover, the performance of penance plays a part in satisfying or atoning for the temporal punishment due to sin. It's interesting to note that in the early Church, there was more of a concern for atoning immediately for temporal punishment, the justice factor to sin that remains after the guilt and eternal punishment for sin is forgiven. This allowed for a meritorious offering of penance in this life instead of waiting to atone for the remaining temporal punishment in Purgatory. So, we had penances of much greater length and intensity which more closely corresponded to the gravity of the sin itself. Today, penances given after Confession are lighter and, if nothing else, this gives us all the more reason to make sure that in love and in proper attitude we perform the penance, that act of atonement, given to us by the priest.

In short, Confession is one of the only no-lose situations we have in this life. We enter the confessional with sin, and we leave it with a clean spiritual slate and the sacramental grace to keep it clean. We lose nothing of the good we have done, but only remove the bad we have done, which is in itself a meritorious act. I use the example in class of a student who takes four exams in a class and flunks all four exams. But on the final exam of the course, he gets an A. Confession is like the teacher forgetting the four Fs and remembering only the A on the final, and giving the student an A grade for the entire course. (But I must be quick to remind my students that my personal grading policy has not yet quite reached the mercy level found in the sacrament of Reconciliation.)

Family Conversion and Reconciliation

In terms of family conversion and reconciliation, we must again seek to incorporate a gradual increase of greater faith, prayer, fasting and penance, as well as a central focus on the family reception of the sacrament of Confession. And the best way to convey the sublime spiritual value of Confession to our children is quite obviously *by example*. How we speak about the sacrament at home and, far more importantly, how frequently we receive the sacrament relays to our children beyond anything else its proper place of high priority in their lives. And the fruits of this sacrament for the family are not just personal. As we said before, there is always a social flowering of personal conversion. The spiritual effects of each individual family member's reconciliation with Christ and the Church will certainly begin to show fruits in all the horizontal family relationships. The change brought about by grace is gradual but real in the family and individual members will begin to manifest the gradual but real effects of grace perfecting nature in the authentic Christian transformation process of grace. Personal conversion blossoms into family conversion, and family conversion shows itself daily in the smallest interactions between family members in the most profound domestic acts of sacrifice, in life vocations, and in a newfound family peace.

To accentuate the family incorporation of the Medjugorje call to conversion I just want to make two practical suggestions regarding the family celebration of Confession. First of all, I suggest making the family trip to the medicine box together, to go to Confession as a family, and to schedule a time when that's possible. And this avoids the one-sided effort for reconciliation. There may be two family members in a state of quarrel, and one will receive the sacrament and have the new disposition for reconciliation in the relationship with the other family member, but it is stifled because it's only a unilateral effort unmatched by the other family member. And although the sacrament doesn't guarantee this, it surely makes it much more probable that, if both receive the sacrament, there will be reconciliation on both sides in family relationships, because both members are going to receive the grace of reconciliation with each other that comes with a mutual reconciliation with Christ.

So, a family trip to Confession is of great domestic benefit.

Obviously this can be done during the regularly scheduled times for Confession. The respective frequency for receiving the sacrament of Reconciliation will also differ among family members. For example, while we as a family (those of age) will go to Confession every two weeks, I personally prefer a weekly reception of the sacrament because of my leading role in the sin category in our domestic Church. So while individual preferences will differ as to how often to receive the sacrament, it's still beneficial when a family trip to the medicine box is possible.

One practical difficulty that arises is that Confession is usually offered at most parishes on Saturday afternoons, which is prime family time, and it is difficult to go when the scheduled hours coincide with other family obligations. And so if the family can't make it during the scheduled time, I suggest setting up a weekly, bi-weekly, or monthly appointment with the parish priest for family Confessions. In fact, it's a reassurance to our priests of the value of this sacrament and it is an example that people still see this as important. Most parish priests I think would be receptive to the idea of a family trip to Confession outside of the regular schedule. I was once asked by a group of priests and seminarians, "How can the priesthood better serve the laity today?" And one practical point I suggested was the addition of scheduled Confession times for the parish. If we commit a sin on Monday we have the tendency to carry that sin with us until Saturday. Sometimes that's fine because the sin is not serious, but if it's a serious offense, or secondarily, if it's something that's heavy on the heart, then it's much better to have the sin removed. Offering an hour or two in the confessional during mid-week would be a real blessing for the laity and could also make consistent family trips to the confessional more possible.

A second practical suggestion in implementing the family process of conversion, the process of repenting and believing, is simply the reminder of the importance of the example of parents in saying the words "I'm sorry" to their children when it is called for. I mean, specifically, the willingness and the practice of parents to tell their children they're sorry when they have failed them in some clear way, when they have lacked a proper parental response of love in a given situation. This in no way takes away from proper parental authority. This simply illustrates the truth that Mommy and Daddy, just like the children, need the forgiveness of God. We sin, we make mistakes, and we need to repent as well. I think when there's the hesitancy of parents to tell their children, in appropriate cases, "I'm sorry, I've done wrong, I've made a bad judgment," then we fail to offer our children the example *closest to home* of the need to ask forgiveness for our shortcomings which is that domestic sacramental that can lead them to the sacrament of Confession. When we admit to our children that we don't always make a prudential judgment even though we do pretty well, we try to pray, we try to use the sacrament of Matrimony but we still make mistakes and we're sorry, then we add to the proper formation of conscience of our children. At the same time, we call them on to the selfsame practice. We teach them by example that when we do things wrong in the family, we've got to confess to one another and ask for forgiveness. Further, it is beneficial not only to express sorrow, but to say that this is something that Dad or Mom will confess during our next family trip to Confession. I think this is of particular value when younger children are involved. This can be helpful in forming the conscience at home and letting the children know that they, too, must say "I'm sorry" not only to the other family members, but to God Himself in the confessional. They, too, must confess sins committed against the family during the family trip to the medicine box, as an ordinary part of their Christian sacramental life.

Summary

In this combination of family trips to Confession and the general practice of asking forgiveness in our family settings, we bring the Medjugorje call of conversion to the inner recesses of our family life. Let me conclude with one of the Blessed Mother's general calls to conversion which, if nothing else, shows how crucial conversion is to the overall message of Medjugorje and how much we, as a human family and as individual families, are in need of examining the direction of our hearts and of changing the direction of our hearts in the never-ending earthly process of Christian conversion. The Madonna of Medjugorje tells us:

> The only word I wish to speak of is the conversion of the whole world. I wish to speak it to you so that you can speak it to the whole world. I ask nothing but conversion. It is my desire . . . Be converted; leave everything. That comes from conversion. Good-bye now, and may God be with you (April 20, 1983).

Chapter 7

Peace and the Family

Dear children, I am calling you to peace. Live peace in your heart and in your surroundings, so that all may recognize the peace which does not come from you, but from God. . . . Celebrate the birth of Jesus with my peace, the peace with which I come as your Mother, the Queen of Peace. Today I am giving you my special blessing. Carry it to every creature so that each one may have peace. Thank you for having responded to my call (December 25, 1988).

The reception of God's peace, the peace of Christ in the heart obtained through Mary, Queen of Peace, is the pre-eminent, the most crucial and penetrating message of the entire Medjugorje event. We see in her title, the Queen of Peace, and her request that June 25th be celebrated as the Feast of the Queen of Peace, that the theme of peace, which is at the heart of her whole Marian message to the modern world, is truly crystallized in this Medjugorje message. It is a peace that, as the above message notes, cannot come from us, but from God alone. It is a spiritual peace that must be brought by us, her vessels of peace, to every creature so that "each one may have peace." I would like to discuss, first of all, the theme of peace in the general Medjugorje call. Then, I'll consider how that peace must filter into family life, the family application of Mary's call to peace. Further I want to examine the effects of Marian consecration as "the crowning of family peace." And lastly, the theme of chastisement will be treated and how the message of chastisement is to be properly understood in the context of the message of peace.

Medjugorje Call to Peace

The general Medjugorje call to peace is not so much a question of means, as we've talked about in the other chapters, but it is rather *the fruit* of living the overall message of Medjugorje. On three occasions, witnessed by hundreds of people, the word "mir," the Croatian word for "peace," was written in the sky in Medjugorje. This one word chosen by the Madonna well expresses the nucleus of what she is trying to accomplish at Medjugorje and throughout the entire world. Early in the apparitions, on the third day, Marija received an apparition of the Madonna weeping with the Cross in the background. The Blessed Mother exclaimed:

> Peace, peace, peace . . . nothing but peace. Men must be reconciled with God and with each other. For this to happen, it is necessary to believe, to pray, to fast, to go to Confession. Go in God's peace (June 26, 1981).

This message reveals the means to spiritual peace, which is the ultimate goal of Medjugorje: greater faith, greater prayer, greater fasting, greater penance, and greater conversion. And scripturally we know that peace is the spiritual fruit of conversion. We can say theologically that the peace of Christ is the fruit of the indwelling of the Holy Spirit in the souls of the just, as St. Paul says in Galatians 5. Wherever we have the presence of the Holy Spirit, especially when we're talking about the indwelling that accompanies sanctifying grace, we also have the Father and the Son dwelling within. And so interior peace in its most profound expression is the Holy Trinity dwelling within the soul, which in a real way is a foretaste of the eternal peace experienced in Heaven. It has been said in a figurative sense that Heaven and Hell start here, and that is true in the sense that we begin the life of grace here on earth. And although still we experience the valley of tears, which is certainly part of the Christian life on earth, there is nonetheless a lasting spiritual peace that is a foretaste of the peace that is to come in Heaven. With the Trinity dwelling in the souls of the just, we become walking tabernacles of God; we imitate the Virgin herself in allowing Christ to become present in the humble stable of our hearts. And where Christ is, there too is His peace, as proclaimed by the myriad of angels to the shepherds at the nativity of our Saviour, "Glory to God in the highest, and peace on earth among men of good will" (Lk 1:14). Contrariwise, a life outside of sanctifying grace, without the peace of Christ in the soul, is a foretaste of Hell. Hell is eternal separation from God. We get a foretaste of Hell in this life with the absence of Christ and of the Holy Spirit in the soul.

The Gospa's call of peace is not primarily a social call. It is not even primarily a global call. It is primarily a call for the *spiritual interior peace of Jesus Christ in the heart.* This primary call certainly has social and global ramifications. But the first call of Medjugorje is the interior peace of Christ in the heart. It is sometimes difficult for us in the Western World to realize that it's not so much a social call as it is a spiritual call with social effects. Early in the process of interviewing the visionaries, Mirjana was interviewed by Father Vlasic and he asked her the question: "So the message of the Madonna is a message of peace?" And Mirjana responded: "Yes. Primarily peace of the soul. If a person has it in his soul, he is surrounded by it" (January 10, 1983). Also, in a September 1986 message the Blessed Mother affirms that once we obtain the spiritual peace of Christ through greater prayer, fasting, penance and conversion, then it is to be spread to others in a more social dimension:

Dear children, through your own peace, I am calling you to help others to see and to start searching for peace. Dear children, you are at peace and, therefore, you cannot comprehend the absence of peace. Again I am calling you so that through prayer and your life you will help to destroy everything evil in people and uncover the deception that Satan is using (September 25, 1986).

The heart of the Medjugorje message of peace is that if we are going to have social peace and ultimately global peace, it must be based on the interior spiritual peace of Christ as its foundation. Does this mean we don't seek any social means to peace? No. It means that global peace is not going to happen without the prior spiritual peace of Christ as its foundation.

Family Peace

How does the message of peace apply to family life? Well, the first flowering of the interior peace of Christ is a family flowering. We can say that the spreading of Christ's peace must first begin at home. In a July 1986 message the Virgin said:

> Dear children! Hatred gives birth to divisions and does not regard anyone or anything. I call you always to bring harmony and peace. Especially, dear children, *in the place where you live*, act with love [emphasis added] (July 31, 1986).

Furthermore, in December 1984 the Blessed Virgin states:

> First of all, begin to love your own family, everyone in the parish, and then you'll be able to love and accept all who are coming over here (December 13, 1984).

So, the first blossoming of the spiritual peace of Christ is to take place in the family, and our own home is ironically sometimes the most difficult place for peace to be spread. Oftentimes to be the vessel of Christ's peace to our brother or sister or husband or children or parent is a special challenge, requiring a particular sacrifice of love. Sometimes, our own relatives are the least disposed to receiving the Gospel of Jesus from someone in their own family. Our Lord certainly experienced this in His inability to be fully a "prophet in His own country." That is why the Blessed Mother rarely calls us to *speak* of her message of peace; rather, she underscores over and over again the call to *live* the message of peace. She knows that peace by example is the true conveyor of the spiritual peace of Christ, and this especially holds true within the family.

In recent interviews, the visionaries have been very adamant about the Family Rosary as a major instrument both in protecting the family against the attack of Satan and as a powerful instrument in bringing peace to the domestic Church. This same emphasis surfaces in different interviews of Mirjana, Ivanka, Ivan, Marija and Vicka. They all stressed that the foremost means to family peace is generally prayer and fasting, but specifically the Family Rosary. The consistent praying of the Family Rosary remains an incredible agent for bringing and sustaining the peace of Christ in our homes.

Family Consecration

A crowning means of peace for the family is the act of family consecration. Several converging streams of Church renewal right now are calling, in a complimentary way with Medjugorje, for a consecration of families to the Hearts of Jesus and Mary. From early on in Medjugorje, the Blessed Mother, especially through Jelena, asked families to consecrate themselves daily to the Sacred Heart of Jesus and to the Immaculate Heart of Mary. In 1983, the Mother of Jesus revealed to Jelena specific prayers of consecration to both the Sacred Heart and the Immaculate Heart. Obviously no one is limited to any particular form of consecration, but the transmission of these consecration prayers to Jelena reveals the importance of the act of consecration in the mind and heart of the Blessed Virgin.

In the October 1988 message, she spoke about consecration to the Heart of Jesus and to her Immaculate Heart as a daily event. In this message Our Lady invites not only individuals, but also families and even parishes to give themselves in the act of consecration:

> Dear children, my invitation that you live the messages which I am giving you is a daily one. Especially, little children, because I want to draw you closer to the Heart of Jesus. Therefore, little children, I am inviting you today to the prayer of consecration to Jesus, my dear Son, so that each of your hearts may be His. And then I am inviting you to consecration to my Immaculate Heart. I want you to consecrate yourselves as persons, as families, and as parishes, so that all belongs to God through my hands. Therefore, dear children, pray that you comprehend the greatness of this message which I am giving you. I do not want anything for myself, rather all for the salvation of your souls. Satan is strong and therefore, little children, by constant prayer, press tightly against my motherly heart. Thank you for having responded to my call (October 25, 1988).

We have here a penetrating message reminding us that the ultimate goal of consecration is always directed to the person of Jesus Christ and that the Blessed Mother is the *God-given means* to a greater union with Jesus Christ as well as the source of motherly protection against Satan. The last line of this message is sublimely endearing with the invitation to press tightly against Mary's motherly heart for protection against Satan, a pressing effected by vigilant prayer.

The Nature of Consecration

What is the nature of consecration? Consecration fundamentally is a promise of love that gives all that we are and all that we do to Jesus through Mary's immaculate hands. Now, the Heart of Jesus we know traditionally is the symbol and channel of His infinite mercy and love. Secondly, it is a symbol of the suffering that He endures because of the sins that continue in His Body. There's no question theologically that the same Christ who paid the price through His Passion, Death and Resurrection, and who ascended to the right hand of the Father, is at the same time still suffering because of the sins in the Body. He is suffering now and He continues to suffer until the sins of the Body are removed. As long as there's sin in the Body, Christ the Head will suffer. That is why in Colossians 1, we are called to "make up what is lacking in the sufferings of Christ" (Col 1:22). So, the Heart of Jesus is encircled by thorns reminding us that this is a heart that suffers as long as we continue to sin.

The Immaculate Heart of Mary is the stainless, perfect channel to the Sacred Heart of Jesus. Her Heart is the God-appointed channel to the Sacred Heart, and the providential route by which we are to tap the infinite graces and mercy of the Divine Heart of Jesus. This is captured in Mary's role as Mediatrix of All Graces, as well as the title granted to her by Pope John Paul II as the Mediatrix of Mercy.

In the message of Fatima, the Blessed Mother said that *God wished* to establish devotion to her Immaculate Heart. She was not doing her own bidding for veneration but was acting as an obedient daughter of the Father in establishing devotion to her Heart. It was the expressed will of God. So, the Heart of Mary is an immaculate channel to the Heart of her Son. And again, as St. Maximilian Kolbe says, to properly respect the way God came to us, which was through this sinless channel, we should use the same sinless channel in our journey back to Him, the channel of the Immaculata.

The Fruits of Family Consecration

There are several profound fruits to Marian consecration. First of all, there is what the Holy Father would call the gift of self-donation, that is, we humbly give ourselves and our families back to our Creator, to Him who is the source of our life, our breath, our faith, and our family life. A consecration says, "All that I have I give back to you." So, it doesn't start where we often start, which is with petition, it starts with thanksgiving and self-donation. It is the offering of ourselves and our families to God.

Further, consecration is a tremendously powerful source of spiritual protection for our families. When we consecrate our families to Mary, and we explicitly say, "All that we are is yours to be given by you to Jesus Christ," then that act of the will has a spiritual power (as, for example, the act of the will that unites a couple for a lifetime, or the act of the will in which an individual offers himself entirely to the Church in the form of priesthood or religious life). A willed commitment has tremendous spiritual consequences, as when we start each day saying, "We are the Blessed Virgin's, so that she can give us to God." When the family belongs in this special way to Jesus and Mary, then by our consent they can spiritually protect our families as a reciprocal fruit of our self-gift to them.

Moreover, a true act of consecration on our part allows Mary the freedom to use her full power of intercession in protecting and sanctifying our families. The Blessed Mother, like the heavenly Father, respects our free will. As the heavenly Father can't infringe on our freedom, so Mary, as our Spiritual Mother, awaits our free act of consecration, since she too, to some degree, can only intercede for us to the extent that we allow her. When we consecrate ourselves and our families to the Immaculate Heart, we are saying, "I allow Mary complete freedom to use all her power of intercession to sanctify and protect myself and my family." A consecration says, "We want you, Mother, and your maximum influence of grace in our lives." The door is completely open. Once you let the Mother of God fully into your spiritual lives, then she is going to use everything she has to lead you to her Son. Giving full freedom to the Blessed Mother to intercede on our behalf is a very powerful means of sanctifying the home.

For a further spiritual fruit of Marian consecration, we refer to St. Louis Marie de Montfort who is really the master of Marian consecration. He notes that the central fruit of Marian consecration is to allow Mary to help us to be true to our Baptismal vows. Origen, one of the early Christian writers, said that the whole Christian life is nothing more than being true to our Baptismal promises. This means to be true to the promises we make in the Creed, all the truths of the faith, and to try to live our lives according to these truths. So, we have two options. One option is to try to live up to our Baptismal promises alone. The second is that we can try to live according to our Baptismal promises with the inestimable help of the Blessed Virgin. Consecration puts into action the latter option of trying to live our Baptismal vows with the fullest possible intercession of the Blessed Virgin. This is the goal of consecration to Jesus through Mary.

We can see that consecration, first of all, is Christ-centered, and secondly, it allows Mary to do all she can as Spiritual Mother. This was the very title granted to the Blessed Virgin at Vatican II, that "she is a mother to us in the order of grace" (Lumen Gentium, No.61). Family consecration, it should be added, allows Mary in a special way to become the Spiritual Mother of our domestic Church. She intercedes for us because, in a real spiritual sense, our children become her children as well. This is a source of tremendous relief and support for parents in knowing that through consecration we have initiated Mary as Spiritual Mother of our humble family, a Mother who will be ever actively engaged in directing our children to their heavenly home and the life of grace. Family consecration is saying to Mary, "Our children are your children, and we vow daily to cooperate with your graces to raise these children according to your daily inspiration." Obviously we know that even after we consecrate our families to Mary we still have the nitty-gritty of daily family living in raising our children, but it is, nonetheless, a source of true peace to know that we're not doing this alone, and we've allowed the Mother of Jesus to be primary in the formation of our family. Consecration is not simply a pious practice we perform each day, it is the unleashing of the transforming grace of God.

Consecration to the Hearts of Jesus and Mary is a strong call not only present in the message of Medjugorje, but likewise, in the recent words and actions of the teaching authority of the Church. Pope John Paul II, along with many of the bishops of the world, on March 25, 1984, consecrated the world to the Immaculate Heart of Mary. My family and I were present for the event in St. Peter's Square at the Vatican, and it was one of the most beautiful events we've ever experienced amidst the cheers and tears of over a half million people. Looking from the piazza, we saw people all the way to the Tiber River and seemingly beyond. As the statue of the Pilgrim Virgin of Fatima was carried in, people spontaneously broke out in tears while waving white handkerchiefs and praying through song, "Immaculate Mary." Then the Pope, as spiritual father of all peoples, knelt at the foot of the statue of Mary and consecrated the world to her Immaculate Heart. Everyone present seemed to sense the incredible importance of this act of consecration by the Vicar of Christ.

In his 1987 encyclical, *Mother of the Redeemer*, the Holy Father offers us a compelling theology of Marian consecration in which he invites all Christians to "filially entrust themselves to the Mother of Christ." The Holy Father offers a commentary on John 19 which tells of Our Lord hanging from the Cross on Calvary and saying to Mary, "Woman, behold thy son," and to John, "Son, behold thy Mother" (Jn 19:26). John Paul says we should all imitate John the beloved disciple and respond to the command of Jesus on the Cross to "behold our Mother" by *taking Mary into our homes*. The Pope points out that if we want to be Christian disciples, then we should imitate the beloved disciple of the Gospel, and that is John. Jesus from the Cross says: "Behold your Mother." It is not an obscure invitation, it is not asking "Are you interested in having my Mother as your Mother?" Rather, it states the theological fact, "Behold your Mother." Our question then should not be, "Is Mary our Mother?", but rather, "How do we properly 'behold our Mother?' " How do we properly obey this command of Christ? The Holy Father's answer: by imitating St. John. What does the beloved disciple do? He takes Mary into his home. As the Pope states:

> The Marian dimension of the life of a disciple is expressed in a special way precisely through this filial entrusting to the Mother of Christ . . . Entrusting himself to Mary in a filial manner, the Christian, like the Apostle John, welcomes the Mother of Christ "into his own home" (*Mother of the Redeemer*, No. 45).

In Polish, the native language of the Pope, it's interesting to note that the word "consecration" holds the same meaning as the word "entrustment." So, it's another way of speaking of a complete gift of self to Mary. The Pope also explains the meaning of the word "home." When John invites Mary "into his home," that "home" is symbolic of the spiritual life, the interior life. So, when John brings Mary "into his home" he brings Mary in as Mother of his spiritual life. And he underlines this as the Marian dimension of being a disciple of Christ, which infers that it is a central call to *all* disciples of Christ. It is the necessary Marian aspect in being a true disciple of Christ, this entrusting, this allowing Mary into our spiritual life.

Entrusting our entire families to the Mother of Christ means inviting Mary anew daily into the spiritual lives of each and every family member. And once we invite Mary into the interior lives of our family members, she, like a good mother, is going to do some serious tidying up. She will effect a new order and a new peace in our interior homes to the extent that we permit and cooperate with her interior directives.

The Pope's very motto "Totus Tuus" (Latin for "entirely or completely yours"), is taken from the first two words of Saint Louis Marie de Montfort's total consecration to Mary which the Pope makes every day. So, in what other way could this Pope call us to join him in saying daily, "We are entirely yours, O Mary"?

The following prayer is a prayer of family consecration to the Sacred Heart of Jesus and to the Immaculate Heart of Mary, written by Pope John Paul II himself in 1983 during the Holy Year of Redemption. And tragically, I do not think it has ever before been published in English. I've seen it in Italian, and even in Croatian, but evidently it hasn't been translated into English or at least it has not been well promulgated. So, I want to offer my wife's humble translation from the Italian. And I think it is an ideal family prayer of consecration because it's so spiritually rich, so deeply Trinitarian (and it's also brief!):

Most holy Virgin, Mother of God and of the Church, to your Immaculate Heart we today consecrate our family. With your help, we entrust and consecrate ourselves to the Divine Heart of Jesus, in order to be with you and with Him in the Holy Spirit, completely and always entrusted and consecrated to the will of the heavenly Father. Amen.

So, in those few words, spoken with commitment and love, the family is consecrated to the Immaculate Heart, the Sacred Heart of Jesus, and ultimately to the perfect will of the Father. It is a penetrating prayer of consecration and I think perfectly appropriate in terms of a daily family consecration.

Chastisement in the Message of Medjugorje

Let us now turn to the message of chastisement in terms of Medjugorje. The theme of chastisement is unquestionably part of the message and, therefore, it deserves some attention. But what deserves just as much attention is the context in which any message of chastisement is delivered and how it is to be seen in light of the overall Medjugorje message.

The Blessed Virgin has revealed to the visionaries elements of significant world chastisements, significant global catastrophes that will take place if the world does not convert. These are contained in what are called the ten secrets. We can ask, "Why does the Blessed Virgin use secrets in her messages?" People often have a difficult time with the notion of secrets. And yet there is clear precedence in the history of Marian apparitions for the use of secrets being given to visionaries. Mary revealed three secrets of a personal nature to Bernadette at Lourdes. We know of the three secrets of Fatima, and the third secret of Fatima also reportedly carries a strong possibility of a major world chastisement. In Medjugorje there are ten secrets. The use of secrets can be both prudent and effective because a secret allows us to know that something is coming which deserves spiritual preparation but does not cause hysteria. For example, if the Blessed Mother came to Medjugorje and said that the fourth secret is that the state of Ohio is going to go up in a nuclear blast, the major effect would probably consist of people leaving the state of Ohio. We wouldn't necessarily have people praying and fasting and converting, we would have them getting out of the direction of the chastisement. And we would have a lot of hysteria in the process, which is not the intention of the Mother of God, our Queen of Peace. She does not come down saying, ''I am the Queen of the Chastisement, beware . . . ''; rather, she fundamentally beckons us to the peace of her Son, and as a loving Mother will also do, she warns us of upcoming peril for our sakes. So the use of secrets has a proper role in telling us that something is coming that deserves spiritual attention and preparation; it does not cause counterproductive panic or hysteria.

At Medjugorje, not all of the ten secrets are of the nature of chastisement. There are, within the ten secrets, three admonitions, three warnings that are of a lighter nature. One of these warnings or admonitions makes reference to the miracle, the sign at the termination of the apparitions that will be a sign for unbelievers which is obviously a positive warning, a positive event. We also know that the later chastisements, without having them revealed, are of a more serious and punitive nature. Mirjana has been directed to reveal the events contained in the secrets to Father Petar, a priest in Medjugorje, some days before an actual event is to occur. Father Petar will then decide what to do with the secret. Whether he's going to hit the press with it, or whether he's going to promulgate it in a more humble fashion, we don't know. But obviously the reason for the revelation to Father Petar before the event is to add assurance to the authenticity of the overall Medjugorje event. It certainly gives credence to Medjugorje's authenticity when we know the nature of the event contained in the secret before the event takes place. Again, these are all signs that are supposed to lead us to seek greater faith, prayer, fasting, and conversion.

What is the nature of these chastisements? They are by nature *conditional*. *If* the world does not convert, *then* the chastisements will take place in their entirety. We have the example of the conditional nature of providential chastisements in the plagues of the Old Testament. We remember that Pharaoh could have gotten off with having blood in the Nile, or extra locusts, or a cattle plague, but instead, because of the hardness of his heart, because of his refusal to meet the conditions of God, he lost his own son. So, the condition of these chastisements awaits the universal response of humanity, and that's what we mean by the conditional nature of these chastisements. We also know that the seventh secret, which was a significant chastisement, has been mitigated by prayer and fasting. So, that shows us without any doubt, that these chastisements are conditional. But Mirjana stated further that the eighth to the tenth secrets were more grave than the lessened seventh secret. It seems that to avoid the most serious chastisements may well take a global conversion. We shouldn't need a visit from the Blessed Mother for us to realize that humanity cannot continue offending God on such a universal scale and to such a grave degree without expecting some response from God in the order of justice.

Theoretically, the universal conversion necessary to avert the most serious chastisements contained in the secrets is possible, but in the opinion of most, and I think a well-founded, realistic opinion, the full, necessary global conversion is not going to take place. If this is so, there is legitimate need for spiritual preparation for the upcoming chastisements. This encompasses what I term as the "peaceful urgency" to the message of Medjugorje.

The visionaries further report that they will be alive to see the events of the chastisements take place. We don't need to be logicians to understand that for many of us that also means within our lifetime. The visionaries and most of us will witness and experience these events to some degree. Moreover, the visionaries have also reported that these are the last apparitions of the Blessed Virgin. Now how do we interpret this? Does that mean the last apparitions in this period of Church history? Does it mean these are the last apparitions in this century? To these questions the visionaries usually respond that the Madonna simply said that this was the last time she would appear on earth like she has. And in terms of other reported apparitions presently going on, we could posit the answer that by the time the apparitions in Medjugorje are over, there will also be the termination of all Marian apparitions. And without good reason to interpret otherwise the response of the visionaries, I think it is best to leave the response as it is. It could have a more figurative meaning certainly, but at this point we don't seem to have any grounds for interpreting it in that fashion. So, if these are the last apparitions, interpreted strictly, and these chastisements will take place within the life of the visionaries, which constitutes most of our lifetimes, I would say that Medjugorje calls us with a peaceful urgency that should evoke a response of more substantial generosity in light of reading these particularly critical signs of our times. A similar concern in reading the contemporary signs of the times can be found, not solely in private revelation, but in the official magisterial writings of Pope John Paul II. In these various excerpts from his 1980 document on the mercy of God, our Holy Father likewise refers to a perspective ''universal danger'' threatening humanity, a possible ''new flood'' in our own day:

> . . . however, at no time and in no historical period
> — *especially at a moment as critical as our own* —
> can the Church forget the prayer that is a cry for the
> mercy of God amid the many forms of evil which weigh
> upon humanity and threaten it.

. . . Like the prophets, let us appeal to that love which has maternal characteristics and which, like a mother, follows each of her children, each lost sheep, even if they should number millions, even if in the world evil should prevail over goodness, even if contemporary humanity should deserve a "new flood" on account of its sins. . . .

. . . And if any of our contemporaries does not share the faith and hope which lead me, as a servant of Christ and steward of the mysteries of God, to implore God's mercy for humanity in this hour of history, let him at least try to understand the reason for my concern. It is dictated by love for man, for all that is human and which, according to the intuitions of many of our contemporaries, is threatened by an immense danger [emphasis added] (*Dives in Misericordia*, No. 15).

I emphasize the peaceful aspect, while underscoring the legitimate urgency as well.

What then is the proper Christian response to chastisement? It is important to see that a chastisement is an event either performed or allowed by Almighty God, and this means theologically that it remains within the domain of Divine Providence. Now, whether the act is directly performed by God or whether it is allowed by God as a result of human sin, is as yet a mystery. But I think we can say that a global chastisement is at least an act permitted by God with the overall good of humanity behind it in terms of purification and final conversion. Let's use the example of the father and his child. Let's say the father comes home, he sees the child playing in the freeway, so he spanks the child. And what's the purpose of the spanking? A mere releasing of the anger of the father? No, on the contrary, it is for the good of the child and the long-term safety and benefit of the child. And so the father wants to give the child negative reinforcement for the action. Chastisement by its nature can be seen as a type of *divine spanking by the "Abba."* It is a divine spanking by the Father for the good of His human children. It is a type of severe mercy, but mercy nonetheless, for the overall good of humanity. The Christian must see chastisement in that light, otherwise he or she could be tempted to take an almost atheistic approach to chastisement which says, "This disaster is out of God's hands; it's out of control and even He can't do anything about this." Fundamentally this approach holds that it is completely out of the domain of Divine Providence, which it cannot be.

Even chastisement has to be seen as at least remotely part of Divine Providence. Chastisement rightly seen can produce real fruits of conversion and eventual peace for the human race. This does not mean of course that we should long for chastisements. But as people of faith, we should be sustained in the truth of the unquestionable spiritual principle that God makes good out of any event, which includes chastisements. Through chastisement God can call *all of us* to a new examination of conscience, a new examination of heart that asks the fundamental question that so many of our own age have ceased asking: "What am I doing on earth?" "What is the reason for my human existence?" Is it for advancing in power and position at work, for the accumulation of money for the summer condo or luxurious retirement home, for the greatest possible degree of sensual enjoyment even at the use of others or oneself? Or am I on earth to make a choice for myself that has nothing short of an eternal ramification? It must be said that in some cases only a proximate threatening of life itself can bring this question to the forefront of human thought. And we all know in our humanness the many things that can come into play in this life, some so dramatically that we postpone or put off entirely the fundamental question of our relationship with God. That's why, in some regards, the atheist position is better than the agnostic position, because the atheist at least has to defend this position, to prove there is no God, which is both philosophically and theologically impossible. The agnostic can go through a whole lifetime saying, "I just don't know, I don't know." This can indeed put off the question of God for an entire life span. But a chastisement can return this question of questions urgently and emphatically to the forefront of the human consciousness.

Furthermore, chastisement can be a springboard for a new, more committed and more perduring peace. It can be the springboard for a new resolute commitment to Christ and His Body, the Church. It calls us to an exercise of the theological virtue of hope. Chastisement for the Christian can never be seen out of the context of reliance on and abandonment to God, and it is precisely the interior peace of Christ, the ultimate fruit of living Medjugorje, that spiritually prepares us and our families for whatever is to take place in the external world around us, much of which we have little control over. With the spiritual peace of Christ in our hearts and at the center of our family lives, we have the spiritual preparation for any and all challenges God may see fit to give us. We have the account of one saint who was playing a game of pool during recreation hour in the religious house, and the question went around the room, "What would you do if the end of the world were to come in twenty minutes?" One brother said, "I would go to the chapel;" and another brother responded, "I would go to Confession." When the question reached the saint, he responded, "I'd finish my pool game." Why? Because he was always prepared for the "thief in the night." He was always spiritually prepared for what we can call the invitation to God's "come as you are party," and therefore, he was peaceful about the duty of the present moment, which happened to be community recreation. We must imitate this saint by living peacefully the duty of the moment. But the only spiritual foundation that allows for the peaceful completion of the duty of the moment is the interior peace of Our Lord in our hearts.

So, a Christian should not have a lasting anxiety at the word of possible chastisement. Anxiety is one of the greatest hindrances to spiritual growth known to the soul. Rather, to exercise the virtue of hope, and to continue in one's state in life by responding to the sacrament of the present moment in the duties of daily life, is what a Christian should do. And we have been blessed with a telling example in this regard at Medjugorje. Jelena, the recipient of inner locutions, somehow got hold of a book that theorized on the third secret of Fatima. She read aspects of the book and became very frightened and filled with anxiety about what might be coming. When the Blessed Virgin spoke to her that day she gave her the following message of immense importance:

> Do not think about wars, chastisements, evil. It is when you concentrate on these things that you are on the way to enter into them. *Your responsibility is to accept divine peace and live it* [emphasis added] (1984).

If there is one phrase that best summarizes the entire message of the Madonna of Medjugorje to the world, I believe it is that last phrase: ''Your responsibility is to accept divine peace and to live it.'' Only a very short-lived preparation comes from fear. We may accentuate our prayer life and our sacramental life for a little while out of fear, but if it is based on fear that does not become transformed into peace and a greater commitment of the will to the Gospel, then it is a preparation of fragile foundation. It is for this reason that the balance of the Medjugorje message is overwhelmingly tilted to the side of peace. The message of chastisement is present, but it is offered in a ''peace sandwich.'' It is surrounded and embellished with the message of peace on all sides. If, in discussing or in living the Medjugorje message, we concentrate upon the aspect of chastisement, then we do violence to the Medjugorje event as well as to the principal task of our Mother's appearances, which is to bring peace to the world. Let's look at one of the most recent 1990 messages of the Madonna and observe her emphasis on the primary theme of Medjugorje:

> Dear children: Today I call you to pray in a special way and to offer up sacrifices and good deeds for peace in the world. Satan is strong and with all his strength, desires to destroy the peace which comes from God. Therefore, dear children, pray in a special way with me for peace. I am with you and I desire to help you with my prayers and I desire to guide you on the path of peace. I bless you with my motherly blessing. Do not forget to live the messages of peace. Thank you for having responded to my call (October 25, 1990).

Let us recall in the Gospels what Our Lord said about the relationship between His peace and the world. Concerning the turmoil of the world, He said: "I have said this to you that in Me you may have peace. In the world you have tribulation; but be of good cheer, I have overcome the world" (Jn 16:33). Furthermore, Our Lord offered us a peace that is perduring, not solely a transient peace offered by the world: "Peace I leave with you; my peace I give to you; not as the world gives it do I give to you. Let not your hearts be troubled, neither let them be afraid" (Jn 14:27). So, if one finds difficulty in accepting the call of peace at Medjugorje, let him hear what Our Lord said about tribulation from the world and the perduring call of peace in the Gospels. He does not want us to fear the turmoil from the world; He desires us to have a spiritual preparation that can come only from His gift of peace. And His gift of peace for ourselves and for our families is a more than ample preparation for anything that can happen in the world. Beyond all else this is the heart of the message of Medjugorje.

I conclude the theme of peace with another recent 1990 message, which states beyond question that the mission of the Madonna is to convey to her human family the gift of motherly peace which our present unpeaceful world so desperately needs:

Dear children: Today, I invite you to peace. I have come here as the Queen of Peace and I desire to enrich you with my motherly peace. Dear children, I love you and I desire to bring all of you to the peace which only God gives and which enriches every heart. I invite you to become carriers and witnesses of my peace to this unpeaceful world. Let peace rule in the whole world which is without peace and longs for peace. I bless you with my motherly blessing. Thank you for having responded to my call (July 25, 1990).

Conclusion

Dear children! Today I invite you in a special way to pray for peace. Dear children, without peace you cannot experience the birth of the little Jesus neither today nor in your daily lives. Therefore, pray the Lord of Peace that He may protect you with His mantle and that He may help you to comprehend the greatness and the importance of peace in your heart. In this way you shall be able to spread peace from your hearts throughout the whole world. I am with you and I intercede for you before God. Pray, because Satan wants to destroy my plans of peace. Reconcile with one another and with your lives help peace reign on the whole earth. Thank you for having responded to my call (Christmas, 1990).

The Virgin of Medjugorje offers us the invitation of spiritual peace and the challenge to transform our families into harmonious flowers, flowers of peace that she can offer to Jesus. This will obviously call for considerable sacrifice by all our families through a gradual process.

In our consideration of *Medjugorje and the Family*, we have at great length quoted the words of our Blessed Mother of Medjugorje, and we have also quoted the words of the Vicar of Christ on earth, Pope John Paul II, and his teaching Magisterium. But I would like to end by quoting another source, probably the most universally acclaimed saint of our age, Mother Teresa of Calcutta. She has articulated, in her usual profound yet simple and succinct way, what I believe both the Mother of Jesus and Pope John Paul II are calling the world to: an emphatic need to change our lives in our families. Allow me to offer the words of Mother Teresa:

I think the world today is upside down, and is suffering so much, because there is so very little love in homes and family life. We have no time for our children, we have no time for each other; there is no time to enjoy each other. If we could only bring back into our lives the life that Jesus, Mary, and Joseph lived in Nazareth, if we could make our homes another Nazareth, I think that peace and joy would reign in the world . . .

Everybody today seems in such a terrible rush, anxious for greater developments and greater riches and so on, so that children have very little time for their parents. Parents have very little time for each other, and in the home begins the disruption of the peace in the world . . .

We must make our homes centers of compassion and forgive endlessly . . . Love begins at home; love lives in homes, and that is why there is so much suffering and so much unhappiness in the world today . . . if we are to love one another, if we are to bring that love into life again, we have to begin at home . . .

A living love hurts. Jesus, to prove his love for us, died on the Cross. The mother, to give birth to her child, has to suffer. If you really love one another properly, there must be sacrifice (Mother Teresa, *A Gift for God*, HarperCollins Publishers, pp. 11-13).

So, whether it be the Madonna of Medjugorje in private revelation, or Pope John Paul II in the official teaching of the Church, or the prophetic words of Mother Teresa of Calcutta, there is a call to change our family lives, and in all of these sources, there's no question but that sacrifice is a necessary ingredient.

Our individual and collective family call is to accept the challenge and to sacrifice, each of us according to our means, and once begun, to sustain the process of bringing the spiritual peace of Christ back into our homes. A mother once said that her vocation is to change the world one diaper at a time. We have this invitation from the Mother of God to change the world one family at a time. This is the way to change the world, but it can be effective only through a transformation of family life in Christ. This was the humble Nazareth way of family life; it must become our way of family life.

Appendix

In an effort to answer the Madonna's call to pray the Rosary daily as individuals and as families, there may be a need for review or, in some cases, for an introduction to the basic tenets and manner of praying the Rosary. The following appendix is thus provided to illustrate how to pray the Rosary, which includes the structure and order of the Rosary, the prayers contained in the Rosary, the fifteen Mysteries of the Rosary, accompanied by a brief Scripture verse pertaining to the respective Gospel mystery.

How to Pray the Rosary

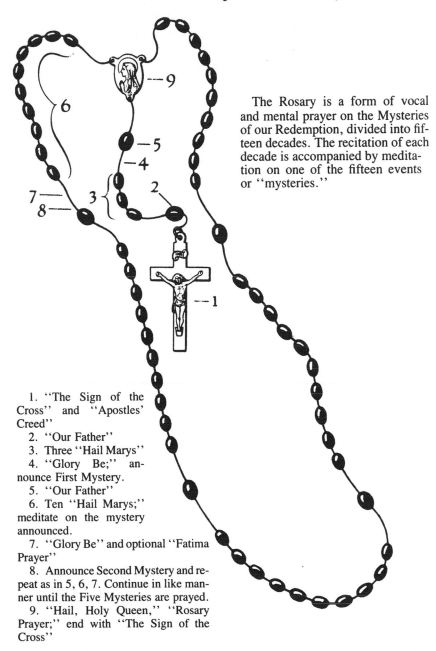

The Rosary is a form of vocal and mental prayer on the Mysteries of our Redemption, divided into fifteen decades. The recitation of each decade is accompanied by meditation on one of the fifteen events or "mysteries."

1. "The Sign of the Cross" and "Apostles' Creed"
2. "Our Father"
3. Three "Hail Marys"
4. "Glory Be;" announce First Mystery.
5. "Our Father"
6. Ten "Hail Marys;" meditate on the mystery announced.
7. "Glory Be" and optional "Fatima Prayer"
8. Announce Second Mystery and repeat as in 5, 6, 7. Continue in like manner until the Five Mysteries are prayed.
9. "Hail, Holy Queen," "Rosary Prayer;" end with "The Sign of the Cross"

169

We begin the Rosary by holding the Cross, the sign of our Faith, and making the Sign of the Cross as we pray:

The Sign of the Cross

In the name of the Father, and of the Son, and of the Holy Spirit. Amen.

While still holding the Cross we profess our beliefs as we pray:

The Apostles' Creed

I believe in God, the Father Almighty, Creator of Heaven and earth; and in Jesus Christ, His only Son, Our Lord; Who was conceived by the Holy Spirit, born of the Virgin Mary, suffered under Pontius Pilate, was crucified, died, and was buried. He descended into Hell; the third day He rose again from the dead; He ascended into Heaven, sits at the right hand of God, the Father Almighty; from thence He shall come to judge the living and the dead. I believe in the Holy Spirit, the holy Catholic Church, the communion of Saints, the forgiveness of sins, the resurrection of the body, and life everlasting. Amen.

On the first bead we pray the prayer Jesus taught us. This is traditionally offered for the intention of the Holy Father, the Pope. We pray:

Our Father

Our Father, Who art in Heaven, hallowed be Thy name; Thy kingdom come; Thy will be done on earth, as it is in Heaven. Give us this day our daily bread; and forgive us our trespasses, as we forgive those who trespass against us; and lead us not into temptation, but deliver us from evil. Amen.

On each of the next three beads we invoke our Blessed Mother's intercession for an increase in the virtues of faith, hope and love as we pray:

Hail Mary

Hail, Mary, full of grace; the Lord is with thee; blessed art thou among women, and blessed is the fruit of thy womb, Jesus. Holy Mary, Mother of God, pray for us sinners, now and at the hour of our death. Amen.

We follow the three Hail Marys with a prayer of praise of the Most Holy Trinity as we pray (no bead):

Glory Be

Glory be to the Father, and to the Son, and to the Holy Spirit. As it was in the beginning, is now, and ever shall be, world without end. Amen.

On the fifth bead we *announce the first mystery (see list of mysteries below) and while meditating on the mystery say one Our Father and ten Hail Marys (one on each of the next ten beads) and a Glory Be (no bead.) Then, as requested by Our Lady of the Rosary at Fatima, we may pray:

Fatima Prayer

O my Jesus, forgive us our sins, save us from the fires of Hell, lead all souls to Heaven, especially those who have most need of Thy mercy.

(Repeat from * for each mystery.)

We may close our Rosary with:

Hail, Holy Queen

Hail! Holy Queen, Mother of Mercy, our life, our sweetness and our hope. To thee do we cry, poor banished children of Eve; to thee do we send up our sighs, mourning and weeping in this valley of tears. Turn then, most gracious Advocate, thine eyes of mercy toward us; and after this our exile show unto us the blessed fruit of thy womb, Jesus. O clement, O loving, O sweet Virgin Mary.

V. Pray for us, O holy Mother of God.
R. That we may be made worthy of the promises of Christ.

Rosary Prayer (optional)

O God, whose only-begotten Son, by His life, death and resurrection has purchased for us the rewards of eternal life; grant, we beseech you, that, while meditating on these mysteries of the most holy Rosary of the Blessed Virgin Mary, we may imitate what they contain, and obtain what they promise. Through the same Christ our Lord. Amen.
(From the Roman Ritual)

End with The Sign of the Cross.

The Fifteen Mysteries of the Most Holy Rosary

Joyful

1. The Annunciation — "Hail, full of grace, the Lord is with thee. Blessed art thou among women" (Lk 1:28).
2. The Visitation — "When Elizabeth heard the greeting of Mary the babe in her womb leapt, and she was filled with the Holy Spirit" (Lk 1:41).
3. The Birth of Jesus — "And she brought forth her first-born Son and wrapped Him in swaddling clothes" (Lk 2:7).
4. The Presentation — "According to the law of Moses, they took Jesus up to Jerusalem to present Him to the Lord" (Lk 2:32).
5. The Finding of the Child Jesus in the Temple — "After three days they found Him in the temple. He was sitting in the midst of the teachers" (Lk 2:45, 46).

Sorrowful

6. The Agony in the Garden — "Jesus came with them to Gethsemane and He began to be saddened and exceedingly troubled" (Mt 26:36,37).
7. The Scourging at the Pillar — "Pilate then took Jesus and had Him scourged" (Jn 19:1).
8. The Crowning of Thorns — "And plaiting a crown of thorns they put it upon His head and a reed into His right hand" (Mt 27:29).
9. Jesus Carries the Cross — "And bearing the Cross for Himself, He went forth to the place called The Skull" (Jn 19:17).
10. The Crucifixion — "And when they came to the place called The Skull they crucified Him" (Lk 23:33).

Glorious

11. The Resurrection — "He is not here, but has risen. Behold the place where they laid Him" (Lk 24:6; Mk 16:19).
12. The Ascension — "And He was taken up into Heaven and sits at the right hand of God" (Mk 16:19).
13. The Descent of the Holy Spirit — "And suddenly there came a sound from Heaven . . . and there appeared to them parted tongues . . . and they were filled with the Holy Spirit" (Acts 2: 2,3,4,11).
14. The Assumption of Mary, Body and Soul into Heaven — "Hear, O daughter, and see; turn your ear, for the King shall desire your beauty. All glorious is the king's daughter as she enters: her raiment is threaded with spun gold" (Ps 44:11,12,14).
15. The Coronation of Mary, Queen of Heaven and Earth — "And a great sign appeared in Heaven: a woman clothed with the sun, and the moon under her feet, and upon her head a crown of twelve stars" (Rev 12:1).

If five decades a day are said, the general rule is that the Joyful Mysteries are said on Monday and Thursday, the Sorrowful Mysteries on Tuesday and Friday, and the Glorious Mysteries on Wednesday and Saturday. On Sundays during Advent the Joyful Mysteries are said, on Sundays during Lent the Sorrowful, and the Glorious Mysteries are said on all other Sundays.